MEMORY'S WAKE

Derek Owens

SPUYTEN DUYVIL
New York City

Library of Congress Cataloging-in-Publication Data

Owens, Derek, 1963-
Memory's wake / Derek Owens.
p. cm.
ISBN 978-1-933132-86-0
1. Child abuse--New York (State)
2. Cults--New York (State)
3. Recovered memory--New York (State) I. Title.
HV6626.53.N7O94 2011
362.76092--dc23
2011023768

for my mother

it translated itself
as it transmuted its message

through spiral upon spiral of the shell
of memory that yet connects us

H.D., *The Flowering of the Rod*

*

You have to begin to lose your memory, if only in bits and pieces, to
realize that memory is what makes our lives. Life without memory is
no life at all.... Our memory is our coherence, our reason, our feeling,
even our action. Without it, we are nothing... (I can only wait for
the final amnesia, the one that can erase an entire life, as it did my
mother's...)

Luis Buñuel

*

Memory is thus a collection of scars of shocks in the ego.

Sándor Ferenczi, *Clinical Diary*

A mother is a hard thing to get away from.
Charles Olson

memory's wake

return

flight

kin

memory stain

burnt

stereograph

"I fall into a waiting tree"

borning house

materials

RETURN

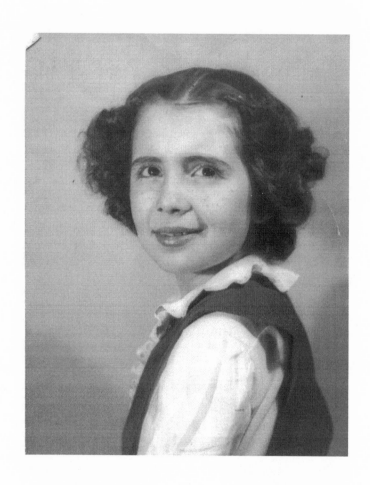

The events of this history are seen to be much more than what we ourselves call "facts"; they are visions.
HENRY CORBIN, *SPIRITUAL BODY AND CELESTIAL EARTH*

recollection, that cancer. inside each

a theater. every head a shadowbox, players on stage, technicians hoisting curtains. ancient accounts rendered on interior walls. histories or what are claimed to be. viewer and performer, one and the same. fade in, fade out.

on my mother's stage the placard reads *Being Scenes from a Girlhood Lived in Penn Yan, New York*. it's the 1930s and 40s. episodes of a life lived before the second war. a pond, ice-skating. Betsy the family Holstein. learning an alphabet on slate chalkboard, her grandmother teaching the girl as she was taught in Wales by French nuns. making hollyhock dolls. the crafting of root beer, bottles exploding. lime satin dress.

scenes from my mother's official history, a life she convinced herself was authentic. which it was, these are not lies. there were good people in that life of hers. great grandmother Anna, uncle Jack, aunt Gladys, aunt Florence. another layer though beneath all that, submerged.

as my mother entered her fifties her kids, my sister and I, left for grad school. the empty nest thing, what we suspect triggered the flood. this is when those other histories, hibernating, biding their time for forty years, came to call. my mother forced to confront an other life she'd kept hidden from herself. scenes acted out behind the backdrop. kept from view until ready or not here they come.

when that second screen is lifted the tableaus are sensational. ghastly. shameful to relate. this is when her waking dreams arrive, the night sweats, women in a circle chanting. *that yellow dress that scared the bejesus out of me. kerosene and mud*, she would later write in her journal. *goat skins. the number five.*

these memories of my mother's preschool and elementary years stayed
buried for four decades. and what manner of self-preservational mechanism
can do that? and what circumstances lead that buried history to erupt?
to wake one morning to a new station on the dial. transmissions from an
undiscovered galaxy. that was always there, inside one's head.

call them forgotten, or repressed. or displaced or pushed aside, the
appropriate vocabulary remains contested. a phenomenon the validity of
which more than a few deny, often for good reason. but not here. not in this
case. this happened. she knows it and I witnessed it, saw the effects of the
memories bursting through in all their violence. nor did my grandmother
deny it. during her last days in a nursing home, when my mother could
no longer visit or speak to her, my father confronted my grandmother.
told her of the therapy her daughter was going through, of these recovered
memories. like when the chimney caught on fire and they left her locked in
her room upstairs, the fireman having to retrieve her through the window,
and my grandmother not denying it, "she was never in any harm." then
there are the letters my mother wrote, notes and poems, she'd hid them in
the house, age seven, eleven. secreted them in the backs of picture frames,
quickly forgotten. surfacing forty years later.

at their peak these recovered memories were relentless. three or four a
week at times. happenings of singular brutality, surreal psychological
manipulation and physical punishments. humiliations, her mother
primarily but to a lesser extent her grandfather too, and that one cousin,
Raymond. hard, for me, not to be morbidly fascinated by the horrorshow.

in offering up my mother's testimony my aim is not simply to share the
grotesqueries of her Finger Lakes girlhood but to present a survival
narrative. a testifying. to document her ability to weather, not always
successfully, that unasked-for rewriting of identity. to invoke Gerald
Vizenor's term, a survivance tale. moving beyond sheer survival so as to

4

climb into some kind of metamorphosis, albeit uneven.

this is also a gesture of thanks. for by all odds my mother could have passed on what she incurred, mimicked and delivered such lessons to her own children and ruining my life, my sister's, in turn. but for whatever reason she swallowed that family curse. let it die inside her as best she could. took the bullet. she's got the scars, they have never healed, but she has kept them hers.

selves lost, forgotten, they wander back in as if they owned the place. rogue familiars.

where did you come from, little detail.

Why resurrect it all now. From the Past. History, the old wound. The past emotions all over again. To confess to relive the same folly. To name it now so as not to repeat history in oblivion. To extract each fragment by each fragment from the word from the image another word another image the reply that will not repeat history in oblivion.

THERESA HAK KYUNG CHA, *DICTEE*

On Sundays my father would drive us to my grandmother's house in Penn Yan, New York. every month or so. we did not enjoy these visits.

my grandmother didn't weigh much more than ninety pounds. four foot ten, born blind in one eye, the other going dark in 1951 when my mother made it into high school. those afternoon dinners. Royal Staffordshire china with Arcadian scenery in cataract blue, ornamental bridges and tiny swans buried under ashy potatoes, smears of applesauce. peas grainy from freezer burn. slices of pot roast pearly gray, fibers on the ends sticking out like frayed wires. in the middle of the table a gravy boat, mud-colored skin thick as a bathmat. if you dropped a pea on top it would have sat there, tiny green planet.

she could be an ornery woman, quick to criticize my mother. my sister and I accepted this as garden-variety old lady behavior. growing old meant getting cranky. at the table she'd ask if everything tasted okay and we'd mumble our approval, sharing sidelong glances and trying not to let the grins enter our voices. were we blind we could hardly have done better, we knew that. so when my grandmother would make yet another, as far as we could tell, benign criticism at my mother's expense, prompting my mother to direct conspiratorial frowns in our direction and rolling her eyes as if to say *isn't she impossible*, looking for signs of accordance, my sister and I probably refused to play. rebuffed her with our scolding eyebrows, *what's wrong with you give her a break she's a little old lady why are you so uptight.*

she'd feel our faces with her hands, tap the tops of our heads and cluck her teeth, "you kids are growing like weeds."

my great grandmother sitting by the radiator to keep warm. echoes of her Welsh sibilant tongue linger in my head. if I dropped a cookie on the floor she'd say "eat it it's good for your nerves." apron and a lap to sit on, chin whiskers. dementia scrambled her mind, she lived to 92. in her bedroom, left untouched since her death, a family of shells on her dresser. three whelks. one with butterscotch zigzags, another bleached and chalky, the third with a mummy skin shell.

what ran through my great grandmother's head when she contemplated my grandmother's dangerous temper, the damage she did to my mother? did she puzzle at the source of that singular violence? how could she have turned such a blind eye, how could she not have known? children were property then, it was not one's place to intervene. but still. what manner of excuses and defenses one contrives to avoid seeing the family gothic.

a print of Maxfield Parish's "Daybreak" hung in the living room. neoclassical soft-core porn kitsch. sun-dappled columns and azure boughs, that androgynous adolescent boy naked and stooping, hands on knees, over a reclining young woman in a bound and rumpled toga. their languorous smiles so unlike anything else in that house of faded doilies, wobbly floor lamps, and lackluster wallpaper the color of chewed gum. they were ubiquitous, Parish's prints, the most popular illustrator until Norman Rockwell came along. thousands of copies of "Daybreak" in American living rooms in the years between the wars. did its image stay burned there in my grandmother's head when she lost full sight? and what other darker brand of world got conjured there? what distortions in that root cellar?

my afternoons in that house were a low-key kind of purgatory. fiddling with the big radio, casting into the static for signs of life, little else but Jesus pitches from the abyss of Yates county. Braille newspapers in stacks, their unknowable language of dots. my grandmother walked fast for a blind person. when she rammed her hip against end tables she'd expel obscenities beneath her breath. I'd keep quiet, she wouldn't know I was there, reading my MAD magazines on the couch. I'd watch her glide and bump from one end of the room to the other. waiting for her to connect with a footstool or the davenport, listening for whatever curse she'd hiss.

behind the house were fields, what were once the family's extensive vegetable gardens, overtaken in later years by horseweed and plantain. when I went back to see the place, after the house had been sold, a development stood there. it was in these fields my mother spent the night one Halloween in the early 1940s, out in the ruins of some ancient playground, wobbling animals on coiled springs, a jungle gym shaped like a locomotive. ran there to escape one of her mother's reckonings. came back the next morning, her grandmother had left the back door unlocked.

my sister and I spent a week there one summer, my grandmother paying us to paint the house trim. she wanted our company, she missed us. I slept in the downstairs bedroom, my great grandmother's old room. unable to sleep one night I stepped through the window, which reached down to the floor, and walked up Elm Street, barefoot, the town asleep and greenhouse humid. Penn Yan little more than an empty stage set. probably fantasized about meeting some solitary girl wandering on her own late night stroll, whereupon I would smile condescendingly upon her life of small town seclusion and regale her with tales informed by my more cosmopolitan exploits, me being from Elmira and all. the nearly sublime narcissism of the adolescent mindscape.

that town no longer exists, not the way I remember it if it ever did. early twentieth century, pre-suburban, a whiff of the small town before it disappeared entirely from view, made over in the 90s with an influx of antique "shoppes," streets widened to accommodate plazas and signage, tourist run-off from the surrounding winery boom.

but my Penn Yan and my mother's are not the same. when I crept through that window all I did was secure a slice of minor nostalgia. when she left that building in the middle of the night one summer thirty years before, the house she escaped was malignant, a poison. just the moan of the late night freight trains, summer crescendo of cicadas, lethargic knocking of my grandmother's clocks, spill from one narrative into the other.

I look around at the walls, the window; it's the same, it hasn't changed, but the shapes are inaccurate as though everything has warped slightly. I have to be more careful about my memories. I have to be sure they're my own and not the memories of other people telling me what I felt, how I acted, what I said: if the events are wrong the feelings I remember about them will be wrong too, I'll start inventing them and there will be no way of correcting it, the ones who could help are gone.

MARGARET ATWOOD, *SURFACING*

That partial gallery. Edward Hopper afternoons, Grant Wood barns, somber and benign. the muted hues of straw and country plaid.

only to find older paintings beneath the pigment, tableaux in blood and mustard. every thorn and glare, each curled lip rendered in a Francis Bacon hand.

my mother would call me on the phone when the memories erupted and I'd write them down. the unfolding spectacle. the shame of it. because it's about us, us humans. we do this to our young. it's not about some alien species of monkey or bat viewed through a telephoto lens. whatever draw any atrocity narrative has stems in part from the unsettling awareness that these characters are cut from the reader's shared cloth.

and to have no say in this spontaneous regeneration! the most banal events would cue them. she'd spill coffee on her blouse and it would trigger a new film loop, of her mother holding her mouth open, forcing her to drink hot coffee. or she'd reach for the ironing board—and would be transported, back to that kitchen, in wrinkled dress, ready for school, her mother's voice, "you're not going anywhere like that get over here," and then her mother ironing the dress, with her still in it. ointments later applied to the burns.

arriving sharp and undistorted, breaking through with icy clarity. core samples pulled from the bowels of the brain, molecules tasting air after eons. branches of the neural forest lighting up like Christmas trees. unsolicited intruders and their stagecraft.

mom, before your bad memories came haunting, were those childhood years like a forest of new growth pines, cultivated in sensible rows? and then the vines came, invasive, tendrils choking trees? old growth narratives reclaiming their terrain. making of it a jungle, with nighttime eyes blinking in the shadows.

or maybe mind is akin to a Victorian house of grand proportions, hundreds of doors inside. front doors, cellar doors, attic doors. swinging cat doors cut into backdoors. cuckoo clock doors, oven doors, refrigerator doors. bedroom doors behind which are closet doors within which are dollhouses with tiny trap doors. dumbwaiter doors, laundry chute doors, furnace doors. storm doors and sub-basement. and my mother carrying a ring of skeleton keys carved from yellow bone, every keyhole mouthing *open me, unlock me*. like Sarah Winchester's labyrinthine Mystery House in San Jose, California. the good ghosts told her to build faux doors so as to confuse the bad. my mother's personal architects, after all those years, had run out of doors.

such metaphors are my fancies. ask my mom today what it was like, she'll just say *it wasn't fun*.

any tabula rasa can be a palimpsest. every psychic neighborhood has its haunted districts. and what comes of identity when the ghosts claim to be more us than we are ourselves? when memory returns a half-century late, uninvited, who is the agent of that narrative? whose hand, brushed in ink on sleeping skin? who knocks, who opens. whose house?

by the time she'd passed through adolescence, so many pages in that girl's life were whited out. stanzas, pages, entire chapters, concealed by the shielding censors. then, decades later, the missing narratives materialize.

memories returning while she slept. moaning in her sleep, she'd wake up my father. *a silent kind of screaming*, that's what she called it, the soundtrack in her head. would open her eyes and find the dream still running, she'd still be there, in the garage, the backyard, being beaten or forced to drink whiskey or made to clasp thorns. all the etceteras, the miscellany of abuse. she would will herself to declare that *none of this is happening just memories Judy these are just memories*. in such moments she was in two places at once.

a middle-aged woman in a sweat in her bed in Elmira, and simultaneously a nine-year-old girl locked in the attic, Christmas day, barefoot in her nightgown. it's cold, she can see her breath, she's vomiting, she's hugging herself, she's sitting in a box.

Marcel Duchamp coined a term for that liminal, indeterminate state when separate phenomena commingle: infrathin. this was inframemory.

Judy never had it any good over there.
MY GREAT AUNT GLADYS

The colorful vocabulary of memory. the engram. the memory trace. holographic neurons. mind ghosts. "somehow spread like smoke throughout the brain."

the brain as library, this is one of the more enduring metaphors. memories depicted as volumes stored and retrieved in the stacks of the psyche. many of the books eaten by worms, misplaced, lost for good. but then others are returned to over and over, the pages soft and dog-eared. and with every rereading the reader annotating in the margins, altering the text.

different metaphors appear in different eras. wax tablets, gramophones, switchboards, dictionaries, tape recorders. the mysteries of recollection and retrieval, shaped by the technologies of the age. other analogies are more esoteric: leaky sieves, mystic writing pads, cows' stomachs. layers of octopi in tidal pools, wiggling their tentacles to get the attention of seagulls flying overhead.

today we speak of memory in the plural, not as a single system but a complex network of processes transpiring in different regions of the brain. different genres of memory. researchers encourage us to think of autobiographical memory as an engagement of reconstruction. not "flashbulb memories," but assemblages constructed over time.

yet so many of hers, to hear her tell them, had precisely that flashbulb quality, arriving with such immediacy and force as to make her physically ill. and in fact one finds examples of such flashback episodes in organic and psychogenic amnesia. (organic amnesia is caused by physical means, like a concussion; psychogenic is memory loss resulting from emotional or psychological states). some argue that psychogenic amnesia, documented but rare, lacks the same characteristics as alleged traumatic amnesia, and as a result some doubt the viability of the latter.

some research proposes that traumatic encounters are encoded in the brain differently from everyday experiences. Bessel van der Kolk's work with brain scans and brain lesion studies suggests exceptionally stressful or traumatic information gets routed differently. in our brains the thalamus, amygdala, and hippocampus work together to process incoming information. the thalamus is like an outfielder gathering information received through sensory organs, relaying it to the infielders, the amygdala and the hippocampus. but if the amygdala decides the data to be too emotionally significant, too traumatic, it interferes with the job of the hippocampus. if instead of catching baseballs the amygdala infielder is forced to receive, say, a stick of dynamite, it might not get sent to the hippocampus in the normal way so the data goes elsewhere. converted not into episodic, narrative memory but getting "stored in sensorimotor modalities, such as somatic sensations and visual images, which [are] relatively indelible, as compared with the more reconstructive and thus changeable nature of episodic memory."

however rerouted, these histories started climbing out on a day she was at work. a church secretary, my mother collapsed one morning and was taken to the hospital where she stayed for two weeks of observation and it was during this time that her memories began to make themselves known. (while she was in the hospital my father telephoned my grandmother; during that conversation she asked, "is it because of me," a cryptic remark he could not make sense of at the time and would not recall until much later, once my mother had had time to more fully relate her long concealed childhood history.)

her head was forced to learn, like it or not, to make room for the new accounts. like the time auntie brought over a bucket of cracked eggs, the ones she couldn't sell, and my mother, seven or thereabouts, knocked it over.

she awoke that night to something like honey on her forehead. her mother, sitting next to her on the bed, cracking eggs on her head. combing the shells into her hair. made her daughter sleep the night that way, yolks drying in her eyelashes.

what fascinates me, and it is an idle fascination, from where I sit, little more than an intellectual puzzle, for even now I can not truly fathom the precariousness of my own childhood, that is to say how radically different my life would have been had my mother followed in her mother's parental footsteps (or if my father's mother had replicated the child-rearing philosophies of his own bully of a grandmother and passed them along to him), is why some will draw the line at mirroring the failures of their own parents and others don't. or can't. why some fathers disappear. as did my grandfathers, on both sides, able to slough off their children and wives like so much snake-skin. (when she was around five years old my mother's father left with another woman for California. my father's father dropped out of view around the same time; he had contracted syphilis, but refused treatment so my grandmother left him. years later, suffering the ravages of that disease, my father would get an occasional letter from him, the pages filled with nothing but pencil scratches.) what makes some men leave their children whereas others, like my dad, could no more entertain such a possibility than they could grow an extra head. why some people like my mother, with so few healthy adult role models, are somehow able to teach themselves empathy, maternal responsibility. the patience necessary to do right by a kid.

because my mother did not inherit her mother's psychosis. it would have been so easy for her to have been a model student, to have taken her family—not just her nightmarish mother but the others too, her philandering, misogynist grandfather, the absent father, the creep of a cousin—as characters fit to emulate. a child so damaged by its guardians seems likely to either perpetuate the same or veer down an opposite altruistic path. to think I was a coin toss away from having a variation of my grandmother written into my mother's personality. the capriciousness of family genetics, the hit-or-miss determinations of identity.

FLIGHT

Greetings from PENN YAN, N. Y.

Liberation is to leave the prison . . . and affirm the history
that was anterior and exterior to the prison.
ENRIQUE DUSSEL PHILOSOPHY OF LIBERATION

late

June, her tenth birthday's approaching, double digits bring her courage. my mother's plan is to leave before dawn, before the others are up. down the stairs, into the kitchen, opens the Frigidaire, grabs some food maybe, a wedge of cheese, pumpernickel, a carrot. wraps it all in wax paper.

out the side door, the one that won't squeak, she'd thought this through. crickets. smell of wild rhubarb past its prime in the gully. remembers Betsy, their cow, in the garage, beams goodbye thoughts in her direction. heads down Elm St., spooks a pair of mourning doves. always in pairs, mourning doves. a jay barks a send-off.

Keuka Lake, the Y-shaped one, a slingshot. "Crooked Lake." from the hummocky bluffs the Finger Lakes might seem like fingers but from a plane this fancy of God's handprint is less apt, the mark "as unnatural as the paws of a seven-toed kitten." whatever deity left its eleven-fingered sign would seem a baleful one. at such a height they appear an army of giant slugs crawling out of Lake Ontario headed to attack Pennsylvania.

23

knows the way from trips in her grandfather's truck, sitting in
the back, with the pipe wrenches and soldering coil, mother and
grandparents in front. watching the road curl over drumlins, south
to Elmira, great aunt Mildred's.

she walks to the end of East Elm Street, left at Cornwell, right at the
Army Reserve Center, then onto r. 54 where the road cuts a channel
through bays of corn. scent of alfalfa carried over her shoulder.

a right onto 14 at the sentinel smokestacks of the Electric and Gas
plant then due south the rest of the way. this girl will walk for three
days through as many counties, Yates, Schuyler, Chemung. fifty-one
miles. shoes in hand for most of the trip, likes the feel of dew on her
ankles.

> her route, part of it, the same hundreds of Iroquois took to make
> their escape 167 years earlier. they ran for their lives too but in the
> opposite direction, fleeing General Sullivan and his "war against the
> vegetables."

> it started with the Battle of Wyoming in the Susquehanna Valley.
> 1778, an assembly of American soldiers engaged with Indian and
> British troops, the Americans outnumbered three to one. when it's
> over 300 of their original 450 are slain with many more wounded.
> only eleven Indians and British are lost. a slaughter. one white
> Indian captain boasts afterwards that he had been so busy with his
> tomahawk and scalping knife that his arms "were bloody above the
> elbows."

> the massacre of families at a nearby fort is formidable: "such a
> shocking sight my eyes never held before of savage and brutal
> barbarity; to see the husband mourning over his dead wife with four

dead children lying by her side, mangled, scalpt, and some their
heads, some their legs and arms cut off, some torn the flesh off their
bones by their dogs…."

this the battle where Queen Esther Montour, Seneca leader whose
son had been killed the day before by American soldiers, lined up
15 captives, stove in their skulls with a war club. she wore only a
loincloth, face and breasts painted in black and white swirls. "Large,
dead-white circles had been painted around her eyes and the eyes
themselves were like black holes in a sort of living skull…" the stone
embedded in her club the size of a grapefruit.

"We destroyed men, women, and Children…."

the girl ducks into vineyards at the sound of approaching cars.
spends the nights in barns asleep in hay and horses' breath. pumps
water from spigots. travels parallel to Seneca Lake, the deepest
and coldest of the fingers, where Indians were said to have heard
booming drums beneath the water. a lake that, because of its high
salt content, and the occasional salt-water fish pulled from the water
there, some fancy to be connected to the Atlantic via subterranean
channels.

recollecting all this a generation later, she says her ten-year-old mind
contemplated the idea of drowning itself in those waters. 600 feet
deep. must have looked a minor wraith, this girl, feet mustard brown
with road dust and keeping to the shadows. what must come to pass
for a nine-year-old to toy with such plans.

public outcry, an ache to command the fecund lands of the
Haudenosaunee (Mohawk, Oneida, Onondaga, Cayuga, Seneca,
Tuscarora tribes), provokes a response from George Washington:

25

"Extirpate them from the Country."

he orders Major General John Sullivan to wage a genocidal campaign against the entirety of the Iroquois nation. the army assembles at the site of the Wyoming massacre. sun-bleached bones from the previous year's killing fields are visible for miles. skulls on the ground with "part of their hair on—the other part taken off with the Scalps—others with bullet holes in, or the Scull Split with the tomahawk."

the expedition getting off to a slow start, delayed in Pennsylvania for weeks due to Sullivan's demands for more supplies. a hundred "loose women" cling to the army, placating the "sexual hungers" of the soldiers, farm boys mostly, from Connecticut, Massachusetts, New Hampshire. even so "there just ain't enough of em to go around" to pacify more than one thousand enlisted men.

eventually the army's brigades are torching every Indian village and field they find.

"the size of the crops was incredible and hardly a man in the army was not amazed at them. Ears of corn twenty inches long or more, growing on stalks as high as eighteen feet, were not uncommon. Pumpkins and squash grew to enormous sizes, some of them weighing as much as eighty pounds apiece. The potatoes were very large and firm and of excellent quality and the beans, turnips, cucumbers, watermelons, parsnips and other vegetable crops here were commensurately fine. The men ate all they could while engaged in the destruction, but the abundance was still staggering. Part of the reason for the quality of the crops was the skill with which they had been planted and tended. The corn was in exact rows, well cultivated; the vegetables perfectly spaced and with no trace of a weed growing in any field. There was even evidence that water had been carried by hand to irrigate them. As agronomists, the Iroquois could obviously teach the whites a great deal."

recorded in an officer's diary: "Friday, Aug. 27. Marched at 8 A.M. and encamped by a cornfield of about 100 acres which was destroyed that night. I myself ate 10 ears, one quart of beans & 7 squashes."

eighteen-foot stalks...

around the time she ran away a ghost story is making the rounds, a farmer who gives a lift to a young woman, raven haired, bone white dress. drives her down unfamiliar roads, leaves her at a dilapidated farmhouse. learns later it had burned to the ground years before, the woman dying in the blaze.

lots of New York ghosts sighted in the 19th and early 20th centuries. "a white ghostlike shape." "a large gray shape." "a wispy white mist." "hazy figures." "surrounded by a numbus." darting balls of fire, "headless Negroes" in the Helderbergs. floating German heads dispensing information on the wherefores of their demise. bloody handprints once a year on the front door of a house in Pittstown. sinuous locks of talking hair fished out of mountain lakes, spilling their secrets.

"for generations one family has been warned of approaching death by a group of lights, very much like a lighted birthday cake, which wander about the fields or so before the death." human ghosts materializing as dogs, snakes, white horses, white goats, rose-breasted birds, haunted cattle. cats.

most ghosts "protect their children or the innocent and virtuous; they cause damaging evidence to be destroyed; they warn people, often unknown to them, away from dangerous places." perhaps one prevents her from walking into Seneca Lake. had the child gone through with it, a new tale would have been added to the mix.

"Suicides were common ghosts…were buried at crossroads with an oak stake through the heart, to prevent further wandering."

>Catherine Creek, the army slogging its way through fourteen miles
>of bog and windfall, through near impassable tangles of spruce,

shrubs, hemlock, pine. bridges are built across ravines for the
packhorses and several hundred head of cattle. the troops wading
knee deep into swamps so dark they hold one another's shoulders
like circus elephants so as not to lose their way.

"sacks of flour and baggage, men, horses, and cattle were strewn
along four miles of misery, and all the while everyone feared that the
Indians might at any time pounce from the impenetrable darkness."
the whole army in a state of "perfect chaos."

"we never had so bad a day's march since we set off, but what will
not men go through who are determined to be free?"

in Catherine's Town an old squaw is found hiding in the woods,
tended to by a young woman who tries to flee, bayoneted in the
back, stripped naked...

the girl continues south on 14 past Randall Crossing and Rock
Stream. Greek revival farmhouses and acres of blackberry, Concord
grapes, sugars percolating in the sun. past the International Salt
Company and down into Watkins Glen, described in postcards as
"one of the most beautiful places in eastern North America." where
auntie lived with her red-haired son Raymond, my mother's cousin,

he with the gun, who played his version of William Tell with her,
sitting the girl beneath a tree then shooting above her head, apple
meat raining down.

keeps to the side streets in Montour Falls, nervous that Auntie might
see her. the town named after Catherine Montour, Queen Esther's
sister, former site of Catherine Town, before that known as "Bad
Indian Swamp."

heading south out of Montour Falls my mother would have walked
past a historical marker erected in the 1920s by the Daughters of
the American Revolution (She-Qua-Gah Chapter), commemorating
Sullivan's grand march and listing the site of every destroyed village.

Odessa. Montour Falls. Burdett. Hector. Valois. Caywood. Lodi.
Willard. Ovid. Romulus. Kendall. McDougal. Fayette. Geneva.
Waterloo. Seneca Falls. Canoga. Sheldrake. Interlaken. Covert.
Trumansburg. Jacksonville. Ithaca.

thirty plus villages turned to ash. graves emptied, contents raided, strewn, smashed. "whether through avarice or curiosity, our soldiers dug up several of their graves and found a good many laughable relics, as a pipe, tomahawk and beads, & c."

a burial ground for Chiefs, each grave covered in painted wooden boxes. burned. in the Village of Chemung "some extraordinary rude decorations" discovered in a longhouse including one "Idol, which might well enough be worshipped without a breach of the second commandment, on account of its unlikeness to anything either in heaven or earth."

when it is over nearly 200,000 bushels of corn have been set fire. 50,000 bushels of beans, cabbages, carrots, cucumbers, parsnips, peas, potatoes, pumpkins, squash, watermelon. apple, peach, and plum orchards, burned.

during the campaign an army surgeon has reservations: "I very heartily wish these rusticks may be reduced to reason by the approach of this army, without their suffering the extremes of war.... there is something so cruel, in destroying the habitations of any people (however mean they may be) that I might say the prospect hurts my feelings."

others are less burdened by remorse. a party is sent to search for dead Indians, two are found. a Major and a Lieutenant skin them from their hips down, fashion them into bootlegs which they wear. elsewhere a wigwam is permitted to stand in one village so as to house an elderly woman and a cripple left behind, but some soldiers double back, lock the door, light the building.

a relatively small number of the Iroquois' fifteen thousand die during
the immediate Sullivan campaign, most of the tribes abandoning
their villages just minutes before the soldiers' arrival. yet scores
perish that winter, the worst on record. five foot drifts, deer
succumbing in droves. women, children, and the elderly the first to
perish. Washington's "war against the vegetables" pulls down much
of the nation as planned.

the Indians had their own name for Washington. "Town Destroyer."

she would have walked past the falls at Montour where Sagoyewatha,
Red Jacket, was said to have practiced his oratory skills, launching
his voice into the cascade.

continues through Millport, Pine Valley, Horseheads. knows she's
reached Elmira when she spots the Reformatory, the nation's first,
built in 1876, its fortress walls facing Woodlawn Cemetery.

Woodlawn, where Mark Twain had been buried thirty-six years
earlier, and forty-five years before that, the bodies of Confederate
soldiers who perished in the Elmira prison war camp of 1864-65.
soldiers laid to rest in an expansive grid of white marble teeth. men
with first names no longer in fashion. Green, Micajah, Fetherd,
Lucanus, Miskel, Aipheus, Byam, Levich, Bold, Ferney, Sparral,
Clingman, Dosite, Elsy, Reddin, Wafford, Enoch, Veno, Zilman,
Able, Harbin, Permain, Lanty, Mason, Bracey, Osceola. Welcome.

3,000 of these "Johnny Rebs" would die in the "Helmira" camp from dehydration, exposure, ulcerative colitis, amoebic dysentery, starvation, scurvy, pneumonia, and smallpox. the worst Union prison camp of the civil war. prisoners rationed to one or two meals a day of little more than bread and water, the same year Elmirans enjoyed a bumper crop of meat and produce.

Prison Camp, 1864. Elmira, N. Y.

prisoners supplemented their diets by thinning the rat population. men caught eating dogs were forced to wear barrel shirts hung with signs reading "I eat a dog."

those with smallpox were moved to a hospital barracks and left to die, the dead allowed to freeze outside until collected. during winter months the prisoners were little more than zombies, "their thin blankets drawn tightly around their shoulders, stand[ing] in the lee of a barrack for an hour without speaking to one another. they stood motionless and gazed into one another's eyes. There was no need to talk, as all topics of conversation had long since been exhausted."

1,200 of the sickest men are sent south to Baltimore in exchange for Union prisoners of war. they are "a ghastly tide, with skeleton bodies and lusterless eyes, and brains bereft of but one thought, and hearts purged of all feelings but one—the thought of freedom, the love of home."

a carnival atmosphere sprouting outside the prison walls where
vendors hawk "ginger cakes, lemonade, peanuts, crackers, beer, and
whiskey." observatory towers are built overlooking the camp walls,
the public charged ten cents apiece for "a fine view of the Rebel
Prisoners."

when she comes to the Chemung river she crosses Walnut St. Bridge,
a few blocks from her destination. great Aunt Mildred's house, set in
a neighborhood of sugar cube homes built for GIs after World War II.

who is standing now at the front door. arms folded and frowning at
this girl with straw in her hair, walking up her sidewalk.

—what are you doing here.

and

—what will they think of me that you chose to come here.

that afternoon her grandfather collects the child, lifting her into the
back of the truck, hands firm under her arms.

on the return trip her eyes take in the same landmarks but they are
different this time around, enriched through intimacy. that cane
rocking chair on that farmhouse porch, those patches of roadside
daylily, that smokehouse, that cornfield, that barbershop pole, that
dirt yard with the ground packed hard and the porch run amok with
chickens. they know her this time around. you again.

history, an attention to echoes. any landscape, any house or field,
portals into submerged narrative, layers replete with their crises and
upheavals, common hurts and tragedies and the infrequent blessings
too. ghosts as alive as one permits them to be. the continuum of
one's life, a projection forward into the succession of moments
pooling ever into the present as well as a burrowing downward and
backwards, roots branching threadlike into the strata.

this landscape, with its narratives of incarceration and flight. the
pushing of the Iroquois into the killing winter of 1779. Twain's study
at Quarry Farm overlooking the Chemung valley, where he conjured
a story about a boy and a man fleeing their pathological culture,
murderous fathers. the imprisonment and execution of soldiers in
the Helmira camp.

there were dozens of attempts to escape the Helmira prison but only
one succeeded, the men digging a sixty-four foot tunnel with a single
knife. they avoided detection by placing boards over their hole,
covering it with sod. the ground on the free side of the prison walls
giving birth to half-starved southerners.

lives in one century commingling with, rubbing against, those in
other eras. my mother's flight in 1946 mixing with theirs a century
and a half earlier and who knows how many others unrecorded,
in between and after. the geological record, the buried dead, the
artifacts. witnesses. as are the cells abuzz in the mind's memory
theater. that her story and theirs, Indian and prisoner, is an
accounting of pain and pursuit, of innocents expunged and grabbed
by others with the means and will to bring on hurt and erasure,
points to how common it all was. is. hard to imagine any road on

the planet unbloodied, any acre not blasted from fear of monsters, be
they Indians, children, or private specters.

*

Elmira was built on the site of a small Cayuga Village called
Kanawaholla, which means "Head-stuck-on-a-pole." a "very pritty"
town. "all twenty houses containing featherbeds, buried furniture
chests, and household goods, was burned, and the nearby crops were
cut down."

KIN

Her ghost drawn to me because now, after fifty years of neglect, I alone devote pages of paper to her....I do not think she always means me well. I am telling on her...
MAXINE HONG KINGSTON, "NO NAME WOMAN"

Earth hath no joys but Sorrow crownes and pleasuers mix with pain
THE PUBLICK UNIVERSAL FRIEND

she lied about her daughter's birthplace, my grandmother did, said she was born in Rochester when it happened right there in Penn Yan. this is how motherhood becomes a construct, erasable. one's child written into or out of the narrative at will. flesh made twilight. phantom limb on the family tree.

to name a thing is to validate it, render it true, imbue it with power. so she refused. my mother's grandmother the one to name her. "it's a good thing she gave you your name because a person with no name isn't a person," my grandmother would whisper into my mother's ear, adding "but you're still not a person." no name girl.

my great grandfather owned a plumbing and heating business. his house had grown fat with furniture from customers who couldn't pay in cash. marble-top dressers, an oak bed big as a barge, vanities, dining room sets, curio cabinets. he'd bring his granddaughter, my mother, on house calls, have her reach awkward faucets in crawlspaces. she was good camouflage when he entertained select female clients, it looked less suspect to enter their homes with a child. the widow on Benham Street was one of his regulars, they'd go upstairs while the girl waited on the couch. my great grandmother suspected, would curse him up and down in Welsh about his lady friends.

he caught my mother sneaking butterscotch toffees from his desk once and forced her to eat the bag entire, waiting, arms crossed, until she threw them up. once, when she'd been locked in the basement and tried to sneak out through the hurricane door, he happened to be walking by. "you're not worth the goddamned time

you take up," he said, then slammed the cellar door back on top
of her. a glimpse, perhaps, of what my grandmother might have
incurred at this man's hand. him, on the left.

long-time residents of Penn Yan can trace their families back to one
of the first American cults, that of the Publick Universal Friend.
Eleazor Ingraham, one of the original members, was my mother's
father's great great great grandfather.

in 1782 a traveling female preacher visiting New Milford,
Connecticut so inspired the Ingrahams and half a dozen other
families "of very honorable and Christian character" that they sold
their property and followed her into the wilderness of western New
York.

"she seemed as one moved by that 'prophetic fury' which 'sewed the
web,' while she stood uttering words of wondrous import, with a
masculine-feminine tone of voice, or kind of croak, unearthly and
sepulchral."

born Jemima Wilkinson in 1752 on a Rhode Island farm, surrounded
by Solomon's seal and skunk cabbage, she became the first

American-born female leader of a religious movement, the Publick Universal Friend, a.k.a. the Friend of Friends, the Friend to All Mankind, the All-Friend, the Comforter, the Best Friend. living in an era when humans were not unaccustomed to visions and to whom the godhead often spoke directly, his voice crawling into the ear as one plowed or made soap or writhed on a sickbed.

after joining the New Lights, a raucous congregation more zealous than the Quakers, Jemima Wilkinson caught a case of "Columbus Fever." for three days she lay in bed, near death or seeming so. when the fever broke this young woman sat up declaring her former self had forever departed and henceforth citizens would know this body by the "new name which the mouth of the Lord Hath named raised up by God to give comfort to His people." in the throes of this metamorphic fever in which she "dropt the dying flesh and yielded up the ghost" her brother recalls her proclaiming, "There is room Enough."

"the Fever being Translated to the head She Rose with different Ideas...."

no longer recognizing family as relatives she began preaching within the week, advocating celibacy, denouncing slavery, promoting a doctrine of "love, charity, resignation, unlimited salvation, and good works." she delivered her message in a masculine voice "very grim and shrill for a woman" and with a Rhode Island accent, that "peculiar dialect of the most illiterate of the country people of New England."

by 1787 "Jemimy Wilkerson the Imposter" had two hundred among her followers, a motley congregation of "Baptists, Friends or Quakers, Episcopalians, Moravians, Jews, and a considerable number

of Nothingarians." her broad-brimmed beaver hat tied down over
long black curls might have inspired the dress of her Jemimakins:
Arnold Potter and William Turpin, two devotees, "tall, handsome
young men...with large round flapped hats, and long flowing strait
locks, with a sort of melancholy wildness in their countenances, and
an effeminate dejected air."

her sermons "had but little connexion," displays of meandering,
interior logic and awkward cadence yet administered with
unflinching confidence. her ministry was the stuff of dream
interpretation, prophecies and faith healing. the Friends kept
records of their visions, their leader appearing often in their oneiric
revelries.

Rachel Malin, one of the Friend's closest followers, records in her
book of dreams: *The 10 of the 9 Mo 1815 the F dreamed that there was
a great woman head brought to the Friend and it taulked with the Friend
and sed that it was agoen to have its body again.*

another entry tells of how the friend *dreamed that everything was cut
short, that the hair was cut short, and that the time was no longer than
from mid night to mid day.*

my mother remembers dining in the Wagoner Hotel. five, six years
old. her parents are separated, he's been living with another woman,
with whom he's had a child. My mother's half-brother, a person she
would not mention until the time of this writing, and even then only
casually, an afterthought.

her parents are discussing the matter of custody. my mother recalls
her mother asking "who gets stuck with the brat." she wanders away

from the table, out onto the hotel porch, *my green velvet dress, that's what I had on.*

later: the wedding ring, her mother smashing it, scooping the dust into an envelope, she mails it to him, he has moved to California with a woman with whom he has fathered another child. he visits his daughter just once, years later, returning for his father's funeral. walks with her down the road, squats to speak with her, as if she's still small but she's a teenager now, it's awkward. he has been sending her things on her birthdays, a music box, a two-wheeler. she's got a photo of him in her desk at school, out of her mother's reach, no photos of the man permitted in the house. (as an adult she will try to reach this man by letter, send cards, but will never get a response. he dies, decades later, somewhere on the west coast.)

1945, the war coming to a close. my grandmother speaking into the phone at her ex, insisting he take the girl for Christmas, but he won't, he's in southern California. she pulls her daughter out from under the table where she has been listening and drags her into the garage. commences punching her. "you *ruined* Christmas it will be *terrible* now that you're here you won't get *any* gifts because you're *not supposed* to *be* here."

later she is shaking the girl, nails digging into shoulders, pushes her into the Christmas tree, it falls over, glass umbrellas shattering.

then she is being pushed down the steps, hear head connecting with the radiator, off to the hospital for stitches.

and later, locked in the attic, she can see her breath, she's in her nightgown, all she's got on, that and the bandage on her head. sits hugging her knees, is vomiting, curls up inside a box of papers. much of the attic floor is unfinished, exposed, rows of pink insulation, were one to walk into those clouds they'd sink through the batting into the living room below, the way her grandfather did once, his leg puncturing the plaster ceiling, hanging there suspended as if transported from another dimension. as are these recollections when they arrive, each delivered via some worm hole into the present.

when released from the attic she is sent her directly to bed, her mother wouldn't let her change her nightgown. that night she visits her daughter, sits on the edge of her bed, singing

> "it's 1945
> and we're alive
> and two are coming home
> and you'll be gone, gone, gone"

the two being my mother's uncles, Jim and Jack, stationed overseas. with the war ending there is hope they might be home for the holiday.

Christmas day. neither uncle makes it back to the states in time. my grandmother will not speak to or look at my mother throughout the day.

searching for a home where "no intruding foot" might interfere, a sect member followed General Sullivan's route north through the Finger Lakes but the scars of that campaign made it "too soon to enter the sad, dark, land of the lakes." two years later twenty-five members, my distant relative Eleazor Ingraham included, travel to Crooked (Keuka) Lake, establish a settlement, the Friend's entourage joining them later. rather than camp in the remains of Indian orchards, where apple shoots had begun to sprout again, they preferred a blank slate, clearing twelve acres of virgin forest where they lived in tents, huts. during the winter one of the members, in the parlance of the Friends, "left time." they buried the body in a hollowed-out log sealed with a slab in a grave hacked from the frozen soil.

eventually followers of The Friend would number close to three hundred, settling in New Jerusalem, a few miles from present day Penn Yan, at the time the largest western settlement in New York. Eleazor Ingraham, my great great great great great grandfather, "made the Friend's shoes and 'done' that work for the family." he would not leave time until his eighties.

she lived her years with celibate women who tended to her needs. Indians called her Squaw *Shinnewawna gis tau, ge.* "Great Woman Preacher." after a battle with dropsy this "second wonder of the western country," bloated in body but possessing a "calm and pleasant countenance," left time on the first day of the seventh month of the year 1819 as recorded in the Death Book of the Society of the Universal Friends. (in Quaker fashion, the Friends rejected the heathen names of days and months.) her grave kept secret, rumored to be known to no more than two descendents of the cult.

the Friend kept her garden "in good order." she was particularly fond of girls, "would often hold them in her lap and question them about their conduct or listen to their ABC's."

I like to imagine that traces of the Wilkinsonian spirit, some pneuma or animating principle, lingered in the region when my mother grew up, the way shreds of mist lie in hollows after morning sun has burned off the fog. I like to fantasize that the Friend's attentiveness to the welfare of little girls was present at those times when my mother found herself sitting in compost, molasses oozing through her hair. I like to think of the Friend's essence drifting in airy tones across the northern ends of Keuka Lake, breathing its way into her head during these trials, not unlike how Wilkinson's godhead trickled into her own ear when she lay sweating in fever a century and a half before.

one day my mother's inside her grandmother's arbor in the back yard, playing with a miniature ironing board. her grandmother teaching her how to make hollyhock dolls.

—pinch off the flower. like so. slide it down, over the stick.

Anna, my great grandmother, born in Swansea, Wales. who made
her own root beer, whose favorite holiday was Memorial Day. her
garden was her retreat, far enough away where she could hide when
the husband hollered.

—there now. what a pretty dress. I think she's rather pretty don't
you.

hollyhock doll, stick figure, all dressed up with nowhere to go.
standing in the Jupiter's beard and fading lady bells, Jacob's ladder at
her feet.

the girl leaves the garden and goes into the kitchen where her
mother has been ironing. she has on her blue dress. she's in third
grade, Mrs. Gowntree's class. her mother begins to iron out the
wrinkles, the iron's still hot, with the girl still wearing the dress.

sends her off to school, but she sits instead in a stand of trees down
the road, out of sight and out of the sun for most of the day. that
night the grandmother, believing the girl has had a misadventure
with poison sumac, paints her skin with ointments, reanimating the
burns.

recorded by one of her followers, the words of the Friend:
*oh dear Soul I have remembered Thee and do still remember Thee and
do know that you are sent forth as a lamb among wolves. Be Ye wise as
serpents and harmless as doves, that nothing might be able to harm or
hurt you...*

the damage done by one's kin is the worst kind. when the blood ties
go bad, rejecting their own, it must be the sharpest of violations.

auntie's house, Raymond babysitting the girl. she's six, he's eighteen,
in the service. his friends are over, they've been drinking. he gets his
gun.

—we're going to the orchard.

sits my mother under an apple tree, her back against the trunk.
balances a beer bottle on her head, walks away, ten paces. *he's stiff-
legged,* she remembers, *I can still see him even now.* turns, points it
at her face, holds it there, the others laughing, then fires, jerking it
upward at the last second. she can't take her eyes off of him, can't
move. apples raining down through the leaves. more laughter from
his companions, he shoots again.

another time she finds cousin Raymond with her mother in the
garage. she writes about this (during the worst of the memory
onslaught she kept a journal, part of her therapy): *I'm preschool*

age, four or five. It's summertime. I'm in my underpants and bare feet.
I walk into the back room of the garage and there's my mother kissing
Raymond. I say something about telling on them. Then Raymond, who
is drunk—I think they are both drunk—takes ropes and ties them
to my ankles, wrists, and neck, pulling on the ropes like a puppeteer
and me the marionette. Her lips are close to my ear: you're not going
to say anything, are you. I remember my feet rising off the floor.
Mother says give her a drink and Raymond pours whisky or something
down my throat. His hand is clasped on my mouth, I am getting sick,
I am throwing up on myself, hugging my sides with my arms crossed.
Raymond drags me outside, pulling on the ropes, says don't you move,
don't you move, gets the hose and sprays it at me, hard.

another day, in Auntie's cellar, Raymond is babysitting her. he has
tied her up with an electric cable, (his mother worked for the phone
company, had a switchboard in her house). rain spitting through an
open basement window.

was their behavior, her mother's, her grandfather's, her cousin's,
something in the blood? familial? learned acts carried over
generations? or were they anomalous, freak blemishes in an

otherwise normal genealogy? and what of her grandmother, the only positive maternal influence for my mother, yet who failed to intervene and address her daughter's pathology?

certainly my grandmother's three siblings were not cut from the same cloth. aunt Florence, a nurse, quick to laugh, prone to silliness. uncle Jim, and his tales, he was a blowhard, harmless. most of all Uncle Jack, physically imposing, solid, a man who gave the impression of being able to fix anything. he'd look at me from the corner of his eye, half smiling, as if to say, I know what you're up to boy. the kind they call salt of the earth. he and aunt Gladys lived next door to my grandmother, their kitchen a retreat from the awkward silences and ticking clocks of my grandmother's house. shortly after arriving there on Sunday afternoons we'd run over to visit them, our escape, sit around their Formica table drinking pop from aluminum tumblers. aunt Gladys would laugh in that deep-throated rattle of hers made heavy from a life of cigarettes. their daughters, Carol and Linda, older than me, big sisters for a few hours. that house, an oasis.

I grow weary of these genealogical excavations. tired at this role of biographer and memoirist, what I've become, rendering my mother's life and bits of my own for the consumption of strangers. memoir, I have never been comfortable with the genre. all those exhibitionists enabled by their voyeurs. all those renderings of trauma and tragedy, followed by the obligatory redemption. still, this the form in which I find myself writing.

but what business is it of mine to poke around in these people's lives so, even if I am joined to them by that arcane concept of blood? what right to take such liberties with my mother's history, her family? what to achieve from exposing, in scraps and tatters, a narrative like hers? it's one thing to reference an eighteenth century cult leader, the Friend from the lands of "York State" two centuries past. such accounts are long cooked, have aged into the strata of "history," their rightful place the public domain. but my grandmother's life? her parents? were they to appear here, now, in front of me, could I even confront them about this? and if not, what cowardice, to put it down here, safely, now that they're gone? their voices no more, none left to contest the record.

obviously this pull to tell is borne of some need to acknowledge the work my mother poured into articulating her secret revisionist history. her freaky tale stayed buried for so long before poking its way through the surface. she labored to pass these accounts along to me, and our family, spent too much effort to make clear the details of this occult childhood to let them stay secret.

and I suppose it's a purgative gesture, too, on my part. capturing her words, here, a means of setting them loose, letting them go. each memory a paper boat, dropped in a river, in hopes of being carried away on a current.

"MOM"

but there's more to it than that. in making her memories public, parading my relatives for you, reader, maybe I am simply speaking to that primal urge. that embarrassed longing to sustain oneself into perpetuity. family is such a transitory, ephemeral thing. whether lucky enough to be born into a beneficent tribe or fated to land with a batch of villains, either way the collective can only last so long. ultimately the negatives will warp and the colors pale, the oral histories mumbling away into silence. every family has its shelf-life. when its time has come and gone there remain mysterious photos of strangers for subsequent generations to puzzle over. boxes in an antique store, three dollars a daguerreotype.

one in attendance at one of the Publick Friend's sermons claimed that "She Preaches up Terror very alarming…"

You, who are PARENTS, or intrusted with the tuition of children, consider your calling, and the charge committed unto you, and be careful to bring them up in the nurture and admonition of the LORD, and educate them in a just and reverend regard thereunto: And whilst you are careful to provide for the support of their bodies, do not neglect the

*welfare of their souls, seeing, the earliest impression, in general, lasts the
longest. As it is written, 'Train up a child in the way that he should go,
and when he is old, he will not, easily, depart from it;' and let example
teach as loud as your precept.*

"As loud as your precept."

and how to begin to tell the story of my grandmother, now dead, who must have,
how could she have not, suffered at the hand of her own father. or maybe she didn't,
by all accounts she was the spoiled of the four children, mean, sour, unkind to her
brothers and sister. either way, her childhood history, irretrievable now, no one left
to shed new light on my presentation of her character. and so how to justify this
reckoning? my inevitable butchering?

she dyed her hair different colors, my grandmother, chestnut brown one month,
almond the next, sometimes auburn. we joked behind her back that the grocery
store delivery boy switched the colors on her knowingly. maple sugar candy, her
favorite treat, lilac her signature perfume. never balked at giving my parents money.
once they were in debt ten grand, my father the one who had to ask her for help,
my mother, she couldn't do it. he drove to Penn Yan to ask her in person, this in
the early 70s, ten grand, and she didn't hesitate. she left a small inheritance for her
grandchildren, I put mine towards a down payment, my first home, the most money
anyone's ever given me, this her last gift to me.

I'd phone her on her birthday. reluctantly. a chore. and she was so grateful. she'd get
emotional, so weepingly thankful. I recall the little-old-ladyness of her mannerisms,
sneaking sourballs from candy dishes, hoarding cookies in her apron, setting her
hair over a dish of water, bobby pins strewn across the kitchen table, her fingers
patting down her temples to make sure no stray lock had escaped. whenever she
visited, slept in my bed.

I remember too the books in Braille she floated her fingers across. the Library for the Blind in Albany sent her Talking Books. it took a dozen records to get through a single issue of *Reader's Digest*. she was fond of biographies and historical romance. sitting in her rocker, smoothing her apron with her miniature hands, half-listening, half-asleep, feet dangling, she was so tiny, listening to a disembodied baritone dribble out of her tape recorder.

write a message in onion juice. hold it against the light bulb, watch the letters cook into being. secrets waiting to breach the surface.

THE

MEMORY

STAIN

The memory stain attaches itself and darkens on the pale formless sheet, a hole increasing its size larger and larger until it assimilates the boundaries and becomes itself formless. All memory. Occupies the entire.
Theresa Hak Kyung Cha, *DICTEE*

July

10, 1942, a Saturday, her fifth birthday. in 1844 accounts surface of "Holy Mount Zions" in secret locations on hills and in woods of New York state. "Here occurred very special spiritual feasts and ceremonies the meaning of which is not entirely clear. …"

a century later my mother is being dragged into the boondocks outside Penn Yan to a ritual she only vaguely recalls. because she has only several memories of these gray cloaked men and women it would seem my grandmother's involvement in whatever gathering this might have been was peripheral at best. or perhaps the robed gatherers assembled only sporadically, their ceremonies occurring at the likely seasonal markers. this one would have taken place shortly after the summer solstice.

it's nighttime, a man is driving her and her mother to a large barn. this is a cleansing because she's been bad. that's the word her mother used, "why are you still bad, you've been through the cleansing."

she recalls being in a group of five girls sitting on a table in a circle naked, tied at the wrists, a crowd of adults about them, several dozen or so, some kids and teenagers there too. the adults wearing black or gray cloaks, billowy robes. a cluster of women with gray hair are especially frightening to my mother. a bonfire outside the enormous barn. or maybe her five-year-old frame of reference made it enormous, perhaps it was just an average barn. she writes:

There were five goats, one for each of us. A man killed them and cut off their heads. They skinned them and draped the skins which were wet and warm around our shoulders. The group surrounded us, chanting this, this sound, it wasn't a song. We were still tied to the wrists and gagged. Two of the girls started to cry. They untied one of these girls took her away and I suppose

59

they beat her. Then brought her back and tied her again. "That is what will happen if you cry." They went away for a while, leaving us on the table, naked except for the pelts.

When they were done with whatever it was they were doing they came back and put us into an enormous wooden tub where they splashed water on us. There was a hideous smell, some awful thing in the water. We were standing in the tub a long time. Then they were gone again, I don't know where they had gone to but we could hear them laughing.

After a while they untied us, removed the gags, we got dressed. The person said these were sacred rituals and if you say anything you die. This wasn't the only time, there were others.

in her memories the smells come back, hay dust and kerosene. on one of these excursions into the country the adults made the children sit on a hill in a thunderstorm. *we couldn't see the adults but we knew they were in the barn doing something.*

my mother grew up terrified of thunderstorms. when one swept through she'd get locked outside. she would walk in circles around the house in the rain, her mother moving from room to room, peering out at her through the lace curtains, face lit white with each splash of lightning.

my mother tells too of what she remembers as an Increasing Our Numbers ceremony, though she's not sure where the phrase comes from. something to do with the men in the group and twelve-year-old girls. these two numbers standing out to her as significant, five and twelve. remembers some men telling her that "you'll get your chance" or that "your time will come," although by the time she turns twelve it seems her mother had stopped taking her to these events, maybe because by then her vision was deteriorating. more from her journal:

...we drive and drive and drive...a big wet hand covers my eyes...as we walk, a smell of wood burning—funny singsong singing...I wake up and once again I'm in the middle of some kind of circle...

...don't want to sleep...might wake up and be inside the damn circle again...

...I wake...it's 4:30 AM...sand and water...so cold, no circle just dirt and straw...all in a row...singsong again..."earth to sky"???...

...wake up...hands hurting...within a yellow circle people around me crying out in unison..."cast out the witch's spirit"...over and over...

I've sought verification of these cloaked people but with no luck. all I came up with after putting out a query on a Finger Lakes discussion list were two responses. one respondent wrote, "I'm afraid I can't give many details except to confirm that I have a vague family legend about Klannish groups in the East Bloomfield area in that time period. My elderly aunt is the one who told me and she heard it from her father I believe. Just something about a group of people in robes which she thought were white (that's why I thought of the Klan) that were also 'night riders' and visited my great grandparents a couple of times. I sort of dismissed it because they were Irish and I couldn't figure out why the Klan would be after poor Irish farmers but perhaps the group was something else again." (if true this might have been the Klan which sometimes targeted the "black" Irish.)

a second person offers another account: "As I was born and raised in Penn Yan, I had not heard of any such rituals. I was born after 1948 so that may be the reason. I do remember an incidence though in 1970-1972 when I was living in Penn Yan and my husband and I were traveling from Penn Yan to Dresden on Rt. 54 there is a long gully that extends in the opposite direction of the road. We had heard that it had been a site for the Underground Railroad in the Civil War days. I would rather not say the name of the area, as anyone who lives there would know exactly where it is. On a very dark night as we were traveling to Dresden. It must have been toward Fall I think. We came upon a group of individuals all in ceremonial dress. Everyone in Black except for one who was in white. The robes as her [sic] described them were the same thing. They were on the side of the road as we were going to Dresden. We were startled at the sight but also intrigued. We drove by and then turned around and returned to where they had been. They had gone in that short period of time (about 5 minutes). We looked at the site where they had been and found the white robe and a lot of paper with nothing on it. We took the robe back to our house. I didn't like having it around, so I burned it."

whether the tale provided here is accurate or not I have no way of knowing, although there is such a gully off of route 54 not far from where my mother lived. my father knows the place, tells of how he once heard a woman refer to the area by the name of "Nigger Hill," though the spot is now known as "Freedom Hill."

when I related my mother's gray-cloak memories to an historian at the Yates County Historical Society her response was to nod matter-of-factly, then allude to some of the disturbing findings she had encountered in homes in the area when working as a real estate agent, symbols painted on walls and the like, visiting abandoned homes in remote areas of the county.

I understand, and my mother too, that these recollections, however sparse, of gray-cloaked old ladies and goat-skinned children will lead readers to cast doubt on her entire account, calling the whole narrative into question. honestly I am not sure what to make of them. did they happen? did these references seep into my mother's head from other sources—a television show, comments uttered by someone else in group therapy? wherever they stem from, fact or fancy, they have to be referenced with the rest of her catalog.

*

the memory wars of the late 1980s and early 90s were characterized by a rash of extraordinary claims, statements by children and adults, women mostly, coming forward with recently remembered accounts of outlandish abuse perpetuated by family and community members, not infrequently ritual abuse affiliated with underground satanic cults. the overwhelming majority of such ritual abuse testimonies remain unproven and undocumented, discounted as concoctions induced by impressionable and manipulative therapists and unscrupulous prosecutors. while plenty of clients reported accounts of ritual abuse gleaned from recovered memories, "no corroborated cases have ever been reported and extensive efforts by law enforcement agencies to find hard evidence of satanic abuse have consistently failed to uncover anything." of these there was no spectacle greater than the McMartin Preschool trials, with its wave of testimonies from children who claimed to have been subjected to sexual assaults and perverse rituals. years of litigation and millions of dollars in fees later, all these claims were dismissed in court.

so who could fault readers for their incredulity when considering these several witchy memories of my mother's? especially when they surfaced in the early 1990s, just several years after allegations of ritual abuse were circulating. the rash of satanic abuse memories that came and went in the late 80s and early 90s have been referred to as "the Achilles' heel of the recovered memory movement."

63

certainly hers are lacking in the lurid details of the satanic abuse
hysteria of the late 1980s. my mother's memories contain no baby
sacrifices, no goblets of blood, no cannibalism, no torture or orgiastic
romps. nothing overtly "satanic" about them at all, aside from perhaps
the use of goats and the number five, although such symbology is
associated with a broad range of benign pagan philosophies as much
as with devilry. if anything these gatherings of cloaked individuals
were intended to ward off the evil one, evident in this cleansing ritual
she remembers was intended to "cast the witch out" of the children
assembled. still these memories are the weirdest of all of hers. this cast
of strangers, singing and chanting in woods outside Penn Yan.

my mother is well aware of the skepticism her recovered memories
might receive, and not just these brief glimpses into vaguely cabalistic
rituals but her entire gallery of recollections. it remains a hugely
controversial subject, a legacy of polarizing debates erupting in the early
1990s between proponents of recovered memory and critics claiming
that the majority of these accounts are attributable to something
called "false memory syndrome" (a term which, like "recovered
memory therapy," some question because it did not originate within
the scientific literature and is generally not embraced by clinicians).
while the polarizing literature of the early years of this debate has
been supplemented by a richer body of less incendiary research, the
media often failed to turn its eye toward these more balanced findings.
consequently the concept of recovered memory for many remains
shaped by those early debates where one seemed to have no option but
to pick one side or the other. either believe that recovered memories are
legitimate, or dismiss them as awful fictions.

part of what makes her account so remarkable is that she had to greet
the arrival of these lost memories alone, mirroring the isolation of
her childhood suffering forty years before. in this her experience is

echoed by that of other trauma survivors. "unlike survivors of wars or earthquakes, who inhabit a common shattered world, rape victims face the cataclysmic destruction of their world alone, surrounded by people who find it hard to understand what's so distressing."

as such my mother's story in fact is only tangential to this recovered memory/false memory debate. skeptics of recovered memory would not be much interested in her narrative since it did not surface during therapy but prior to and outside of any counseling. critics of recovered memory therapy are less concerned with spontaneously remembered abuse and more with how questionable practices like hypnosis, age regression, and guided imagery, particularly in the hands of a careless therapist, might promote suggestibility, eventually leading impressionable clients to construct fictional accounts. such reservations are warranted as studies document that strategies used in memory recovery can create memory distortion. yet none of these practices took place between my mother and her therapist. much of their work was aimed at developing coping skills for my mother's PTSD symptoms— the helplessness, anxiety, memory loss, sleeplessness, lethargy. and cultivating too a sense of self-worth in response to the flood of memories she was experiencing outside of therapy.

while hers is not a story of recovered memory procured in consultation with a therapist, her story echoes many accounts of recovered memories that have come under scrutiny. the memory wars of the last fifteen years are like little else in the recent history of American psychiatry. incredible and scandalous testimonies, sensational news reports, aggressive prosecution, incarcerations, legislative change, congressional condemnations, therapists being picketed. and at the center of this controversy are two seemingly diametrically opposed sides, one represented by those believing in recovered and repressed memories, the other by those who doubt and challenge the validity of such memories.

on one end of the spectrum are books like Ellen Bass and Laura Davis's
enormously influential *The Courage to Heal: A Guide for Women Survivors
of Child Sexual Abuse*. Bass and Davis's treatise is successful in the
degree to which it has apparently helped thousands of readers rebuild
lives damaged from incest and sexual abuse. but it has also served as a
lightning rod for skeptics of recovered memory because of indefensible
and oft criticized passages like these:

> So far, no one we've talked to thought she might have been abused, and
> then later discovered that she hadn't been. The progression always goes
> the other way, from suspicion to confirmation. If you think you were
> abused and your life shows the symptoms, then you were.

> If you don't remember your abuse, you are not alone. Many women don't
> have memories, and some never get any memories. This doesn't mean
> they weren't abused.

> If you are unable to remember any specific instances...but still have a
> feeling that something abusive happened to you, it probably did.

for Bass and Davis, the symptoms of sexual abuse are so inclusive as
to typically include feelings of powerlessness, trouble with motivation,
a preoccupation with work in order to compensate for feelings of
emptiness in one's personal life, confusion, difficulty articulating
emotions, loneliness. (to which many of us might respond, welcome to
modern living). it doesn't take much to imagine impressionable readers
who, meeting any of these criteria but having no recollection of abusive
memories, might feel compelled to dig deeper into their imaginations
until they construct narratives echoing the authors' anecdotes. in
addition to the very legitimate need to help victims of abuse heal, there
is arguably a seductiveness at work here as well, an attraction to the idea

of a secret life or a past hidden "just beneath the surface." the authors could easily have refrained from such overstated claims, modifying their prose slightly so as not to imply that buried within the average woman there lurks an inevitable history of sexual abuse, thus supplying false memory advocates with considerably less ammunition.

on the opposite side we have authors outraged at what they consider to be a psychological establishment run amok, where thousands of impressionable clients have, under the sway of directive therapists, come forward with allegations of abuse, most of them aimed at family members, ruining lives and reputations in the process, even leading to incarceration for some. books by Richard Ofshe and Ethan Watters (*Making Monsters: False Memories, Psychotherapy, and Sexual Hysteria*), Mark Pendergrast (*Victims of Memory: Incest Accusations and Shattered Lives*), and Elizabeth Loftus and Katherine Ketcham (*The Myths of Repressed Memory: False Memories and Allegation of Sexual Abuse*) all appear in 1994-1995, providing a backlash to the spate of law suits and public charges brought forth by the wave of new victims. the intensity of these authors' frustration and outright condemnation of what they view as a culture of false memory is legitimate and understandable. as one researcher would point out five years after the publication of these titles, "the evidence that some people develop false memories of horrific trauma is overwhelming."

these studies err in significant ways because they present the phenomenon in either/or terms. the most irate of these authors, Ofshe and Watters, declare that "the practice of uncovering repressed memories...are fads as widespread and as damaging as any the mental health field has produced this century." and when Loftus respectfully but insistently challenges Ellen Bass, admitting the "ideological chasm" that exists between their two views, she concludes that before we can accept recovered memory, there must be incontrovertible proof; until then, there is simply no reason to believe in the phenomenon. a severely logical response, perhaps, but one that inevitably dismisses every recovered memory lacking forensic evidence, thus rendering victims voiceless. such positions present a reductive, winner-take-all sparring match where neither side spends serious time acknowledging the legitimacy of their opponents. when reading this literature it can easily seem that defenders on both ends of the spectrum are less interested in exploring a broad range of possibilities for the evidence they cite and more preoccupied with defending turf. Ofshe and Watters go so far as to admit that readers will be forced to select sides in this debate and that no resolution is possible: "the options for those taking sides in this debate are quite unambiguous: the mind either has the ability to repress vast numbers of events, as described by recovered memory therapists, or it does not."

this divisive rhetoric has diminished in recent years as new clinicians and memory researchers have criticized the polarity of the debate and called for a less divisive, more collaborative approach to better understanding these phenomena. as the authors of one study put it, "a more balanced approach...is to acknowledge that society faces two serious problems: underreporting of abuse when it has indeed occurred and over-reporting of abuse when it has not occurred. Although we view the former as the more prevalent problem, both problems are in need of remedy." in particular researchers have called for greater emphasis on an individual, case-by-case method of investigating traumatic memory rather than resorting to grand claims for or against the viability of recovered memories en masse.

in calling for a more measured response, subsequent research has sought to address a variety of omissions and overstatements in these early significant works by recovered memory skeptics. claims that there are "over 1 million cases of [false] 'recovered memories' each year" have been shown to be wildly exaggerated. others have observed that a fundamental reason for the ideological divide in this debate is that the two sides are largely comprised of clinicians and psychotherapists on one hand, scientists and memory researchers on the other. separate communities that don't necessarily share the same training, goals, or discourse. some have pointed out that advocates of false memory syndrome neglect to acknowledge that many clients who experience delayed recall of sexual abuse have already had some recollection of the abuse prior to initial contact with therapists. others observe that "it is fair to say that the high levels of interest in memory failings may have tended to obscure the fact that autobiographical memory is more often right than wrong, providing individuals do not go beyond what they can readily recall and attempt to fill in the gaps."

most of all, skeptics of false memory have been reluctant to address memories, like my mother's, that have surfaced independent of counseling, or the commonality of psychogenic amnesia and PTSD. not only do recovered memory skeptics frequently refrain from acknowledging the extensive research on amnesia, some publications provide false information. Reinder Van Til, in *Lost Daughters: Recovered Memory Therapy and the People It Hurts*, dismisses amnesia as a viable explanation for recovered memory: "there have also been documented cases of traumatic amnesia, which is a temporary but complete forgetting of a traumatic event, but the memories of such events usually return with a few days. There are simply no medical studies or documented case histories demonstrating that it is possible for anyone to repress years of abuse." this is untrue. patients with PTSD re-experience traumatic memories in a variety of forms—intrusive recollections, flashbacks, nightmares, psychophysiologic reactivity—months and years after the event.

another study suggests that the more trauma a child experiences, the less likely that child might be able to remember that trauma, whereas recollection of a "single-impact" trauma is more likely to remain in memory. Jennifer Freyd introduces her concept of "betrayal trauma theory," which argues that abuse perpetrated by a caregiver presents a greater psychic upheaval, especially for children who cannot escape their abusers, resulting in "betrayal blindness," a defense mechanism in the form of amnesia, allowing the child to continue co-existing in relationship with the abuser:

> It is proposed here that there is a logic to amnesia for childhood abuse. Under certain conditions, such as abuse by a close caregiver, amnesia about the abuse is an adaptive response, for amnesia may allow a dependent child to remain attached to—and thus elicit at least some degree of life-sustaining nurturing and protection from—his or her abusive caregiver.

finally, perhaps most significantly, there are documented cases where people have corroborated their recovered memories of abuse.

where my sympathies lie are obvious. it is not that I do not share the skeptic's frustration at therapists who, willfully or naively, steer susceptible clients into imaginary forests they mistakenly come to recognize as home. I can barely imagine what parents whose children have falsely accused them of physical or sexual or emotional or verbal abuse must go through. the surreal horror of hearing one's child rewrite the family's identity is something one would not wish on anyone. it must feel as if one's child has suddenly become possessed, or joined a cult, and is now lost in limbo as one waits for her to return, back into the person they once used to be. I do not begrudge the doubters of recovered memory, at least not those like Richard J. McNally who, *in Remembering Trauma,* carefully surveys much of the available literature to conclude that traumatic memories rarely fade from consciousness only to return at a much later date. I appreciate such efforts, I admire the scholarship. in the end though it's impossible to match these conclusions with my own observations of my mother's experience. not that it's a matter of convincing audiences one way or the other. this debate, if it is ever to be resolved, will be decided by further evidence compiled by clinicians and memory researchers, not a son preoccupied with being the vehicle for his mother's reconstructed girlhood.

*

sometime when she was between five and seven her mother took her to a doctor to be bled. looking back my mother wonders if this man too might have been one of the gray-cloaks. this was another cleansing because the first one, the ceremony with the goat skins, hadn't worked. she remembers sitting in his office in downtown Penn Yan, sitting quite still as he put leeches on her arms.

during the period when her memories were coming on strong she found a Halloween decoration from her childhood, a witch silhouetted by a sallow moon. immediately she started to tear it into pieces, unaware of her actions. then a new one comes back. from her journal:

I guess I had wanted to be a witch and dressed up in some old black rags. Mother was furious and said so you want to be a witch I'll show you a witch and took me out to the garage. She made me this liquid concoction. I remember it was steaming, it was very hot and the stench was horrible. She almost got it down, it was right to my lips but I resisted, I pushed her arm away which made her all the more furious, and I ran out into the fields behind our house, what I called the three fields—three different acres of tall grass. I hid in the second field by the creek and I remember her yelling, screaming for me for the longest time. But I didn't move. I stayed right there. She made me drink enough things. And I stayed out there all night. It was cold of course, it was late October. I came in just before dawn. My grandmother had left the door unlocked for me.

71

fast forward to my Halloweens on Golden Glow Drive. at nine months, my parents stuffed me into an oversized jack-o-lantern and left me on relatives' porches while they rang the doorbell and hid in the bushes. in later years mom would sew outfits, dad designing the headgear and props. bee, butterfly, elephant, dragon, werewolf, clown, cat, mummy, knight, mad scientist, ghoul. parties with a cauldron, sugar cookie bats, elaborate candy buffet for the neighborhood kids. Zagnut bars and Mallow Cups, orange and black streamers, Hallmark decorations on every wall.

*

these rebirthing rituals and inverse baptisms. the old self symbolically killed off by bathing in a tub of contaminated water, the new self reborn, wrapped in animal skins. and a lifetime later, the emergence of another kind of memory, naked and bloodied.

BURNT

The region had a reputation for peculiar innovations...
WHITNEY R. CROSS, *THE BURNED-OVER DISTRICT: THE SOCIAL AND INTELLECTUAL HISTORY OF ENTHUSIASTIC RELIGION IN WESTERN NEW YORK, 1800-1850*

Unriddle these things.
COTTON MATHER, *THE WONDERS OF THE INVISIBLE WORLD*

what intrigues me as much as my mother's wispy inklings of home-cooked cults in the outback of Penn Yan seventy years ago are the spiritual leaders and visionaries of the nineteenth century for whom central and western New York state became a psychic laboratory. I've come to regard this cast of characters almost like regional kinfolk, oddballs driven by visions who, in light of these quasi-pagan rituals my mom recalls, not to mention my ancestral connections to the Public Universal Friend, seem remotely like family.

"for whatever reason, the New York descendants of the Puritans were a more quarrelsome, argumentative, experimenting brood than their parents and stay-at-home cousins."

there was no stranger place in the United States at this time. New York state, a land of angels and buried treasure, visions and Second Comings as common as thunderstorms. psychical exaggerations were rampant here, expected even, the region's birthright. at the dawn of the 19th century religious and utopian "excitements" sprouted like plantain ("white man's foot") across the glacial kames and kettles of the western lands. these soils, some of the richest in the state, made a powerful magnet, and the filings pulled into this alchemical hinterland were common folk, uneducated, not just superstitious but progenitors of superstition, their exegetical designs as homespun as they were prophetic and cultivated to attain a more perfect, more uncooked, more ancient tasting of supernal rapture.

"there is an over-all, one-of-a-kind nonesuchness that separates upstate from all other land-units of the world…"

there must have been something in the water. by 1820 nearly sixty people per square mile lived in this area historians now call the burnt-over district, named for the zealous conflagrations and evangelical firestorms that swept in waves across the region. prior to the Erie Canal the primary east-west route crossed just north of the

Finger Lakes, and it was here that many of the burnt had their visions and heard their voices. Lyman Beecher, writing to Nathaniel Beman in 1828:

"there is nothing to which the minds of good men, when once passed the bounds of sound discretion, and launched on the ocean of feeling and experiment, may not come…nothing so terrible and unmanageable as the fire and whirlwind of human passion, when once kindled by misguided zeal….For, in every church, there is wood, hay, and stubble which will be sure to take fire on the wrong side….New-England of the West shall be burnt over…"

their families back in New England thought these westward "go-outers" had fallen under the spell of "Genesee Fever," or what doctors called "nervous fever." tens of thousands got dosed with fear sermons by threatening evangelists the likes of Charles Finney and Father Nash, who urged the Lord to "wake up these stupid sleeping ministers [else]…they will wake in hell" and "smite them this night." entire congregations reduced to writing and wailing, catharsis through intimidation. more than a few pushed into insanity.

the "emotionalized culture" of this 19th century "inner space" was ripe for strange sightings, as these were people just itching for divine apparition. Seventh Day Adventists saw the letters G-O-D appear in the sky, bursting from a "serpentine silvery colored belt." odd lights spotted around Venus and Jupiter, as well as a cross sprouting on the surface of the moon. comets, northern lights, and eclipses shook the psyches of citizens in New York, Pennsylvania, New Jersey, and New England. in 1844 a pamphlet was published telling of an unusual shower of "meat and blood" falling on Jersey City. throughout New England there were multiple accounts of "praeternatural happenings": odd thunderclaps, needles and splinters sailing through houses, flying Goose-shot striking homeowners and making dogs' noses bleed. travelers "strangely molested" by stones, dirtclods, corncobs, frying pans. "peels" (fire shovels) and "beesoms" (brooms) attacking families. the frontier a cacophony of spirits, poltergeists, and daemonic companions visiting town after town, painting the mental landscape in a diabolical hand.

historians like Whitney Cross describe these rural towns as populated by raw, naïve, gullible, tobacco-spitting, heavy-drinking citizens (the early Penn Yan was called Pandemonium because of its taverns). in those days science could still be closer to alchemy. the President of Union College thought alcohol in the stomach could be ignited by spontaneous combustion. academics were busy proving that hairs, dropped in a glass of water, actually came alive. doctors recommended that hemorrhoid sufferers carry horse chestnuts in their pockets. farmers claimed to have found the bones of giants rising up through their fields. a Penn Yan doctor reported finding seven-foot skeletons buried in a conical mound near Keuka Lake.

the spiritual biodiversity was considerable. Methodists, Baptists, Presbyterians, Adventists, Arminians, Freewill Baptists, Campbellites, Disciples of Christ, Unitarian Baptists, Mormons, Millerites, Quakers, Universalists, Congregationalists, Shakers, Christian Unionists, Swedenborgians. and their metaphysics equally divergent: espousers of communism, pre- and postmillennialism, spiritualism, perfectionism, masonry, antislavery, temperance, revivalism, celibacy, common marriage, Millerism, Oberlinism, pietism, Fourierism, Owenism, Mesmerism, Grahamism, phrenology, Swedenborgianism, and animal magnetism.

it was not uncommon for preachers to be self-styled visionaries denouncing church government and sometimes even the bible: "stubborn folk who recognized no authority this side of Heaven." nor were these zealots and devotees motivated by economic or social objectives, their motives idiosyncratic and private: "they may well have been as little driven by outward circumstance as any group of persons in history." this was "the storm center." "the psychic highway." the "infected district." some of the most original theological philosophies in American history took root across this region, and Penn Yan was at the epicenter of these entrancements.

"messiah is traveling in the storm…."

even today sizeable tracts of land in central New York State remain ignored, hidden. although this is now the land of winery tours, where elegant homes dot the banks

of the lakes and tourism doubles summer populations, one can still drive away
from the 4th of July parties, the water skiers, the lingering smell of boat fuel and
in twenty minutes, after a few turns here and there onto empty roads, find oneself
heading into countryside that would appear completely uninhabited were it not for
the endless acres of corn.

a glimpse into the area's pulse, at least in the less traveled pockets: in 1990 my wife
and I attended a wedding reception outside Interlaken, which sits between Cayuga
and Seneca, the two largest lakes. we got lost on a series of dirt roads and drove
past listing Greek revival farmhouses in states of disrepair, car engines chained to
tree limbs, the occasional school bus chassis sinking into yards of waist-high grass.
we found the party in a trailer, a makeshift VFW hall balanced on stacks of cinder
blocks. the father of the bride, a man in his 70s, took short cuts to the bathroom by
walking on top of the dinner tables. the best man had changed into hunting clothes
and stayed planted by the keg, his backside crack giving the bridesmaids something
to talk about. the bride's mother had suffered some manner of mental collapse
and stood mute against the wall, wringing her hands while avoiding eye contact.
"Stairway to Heaven," the bride and groom's first dance.

*

and so a tangent, midway through this accounting of my mother's
girlhood, to catalogue several of the ghosts in this land of the burnt.
perhaps because of my family's connection to the Universal Friend
I have affected a fondness for these nuts and visionaries with their
autochthonic theologies, their queer and homegrown christian gods.

this is the land of Mother Ann Lee, "feminine spirit of a bisexual
god" who, when crossing the Atlantic for New York so as to put
the horrors of childbearing behind her, saw Angels hanging on the
masthead. who created a culture where sexual and spiritual energies

where channeled into making functional art built to last millennia, where tongues were spoken in, and sparkling balls of love brought back from heavenly visits. settled the first Shaker settlement outside Albany, the label a holdover from her earlier days with the Shaking Quakers (a.k.a. the shiverers, a.k.a. the jumpers). after Mother Ann's death—her simple headstone stands in a plot just outside Albany's airport—the Shakers grew increasingly eccentric. adults and children would break into unknown songs, enter into "non-trances," speak in euphonious pseudo-languages. episodes of temporary blindness and spiritual drunkenness. travels to the spirit world were common, the brothers and sisters returning with such gifts from their "heavenly parents": "Spectacles of Discernment," "sparkling balls of love," lamps "to be kept well trimmed and burning so that the enemy may not impede our progress," celestial wine, silver sacks of bread, priceless gems, "clusters of white plums from the Angel of Peace." fans, hymns, poems, and maps drawn in delicate hands, and delivered to one another with small tokens—a bottle of wintergreen oil, a dress pattern.

here in the burnt-over district is where the brethren of William Miller convinced tens of thousands that in a matter of days God's trumpets would suck the righteous to heaven and the wicked dead be plucked from their graves, cast into lakes of fire. in the first half of the nineteenth century people had a fixation with the number 1,000. some believed a thousand years of heaven on earth had begun, or soon would, presaging Christ's return. others expected the second coming to arrive any day, followed by a thousand-year run of milk and honey etceteras. whether one buttered their spiritual bread on the pre- or postmillennialist side, many across New England and New York equated the godhead's re-entrance with this magical idea-force. "the coming of the bridegroom" + 1,000 (or vice versa) = the End-times. it was a sum of exceptional motivational power and the area most affected was central and western "York state." William

Miller began preaching that the Earth would be destroyed sometime between March 21, 1843 and March 21, 1844. (his hermeneutic error: after the deadline came and went, he pushed the date back to October 22, 1844). the shy preacher had had a rather standard apocalyptic dream: desert wanderings, mystical tableaux, drops of blood like rain. "I see children of God who [will] meet the Lord in the air where they will be married to him." as the chosen were pulled from the planet the earth would be slash-and-burned, a purifying for Christ's landing. he relayed these ideas to thousands in a circus-sized tent, displaying charts and prophecy banners, lush illustrations of Revelations-inspired imagery: lions with human faces, hydra-headed beasts. some Millerite perfectionists believed that whether one was snatched into heaven or kicked into hell it was all preordained anyway, and thus one's afterlife destiny was unaffected by one's earthly actions. hence some stole goods, others kept "a very bad house;" one respected preacher fell into "uncivil conduct." there were reports of kissing, embracing, and promiscuous lodgings so as to beget spiritual children. an entire congregation in Rochester was engaged in foot washing. "gods Car is moving forward with its wheels of burning fire in our midst utterly consuming every vestige of our old Nature..." at dawn on October 23, 1844, the Millerites transformed into "The Disappointed." some succumbed to mental illness. one man took a knife to his throat with such force "as to almost sever his head from his body;" a woman fed teaspoons of arsenic to her one and three year old children. the Millerites' hunger for rapture reflected widespread cultural longings. before Miller appeared more than ninety cases of "religious melancholy," "religious insanity," and "nervous fever" had already led to suicide in New England and New York between 1815 and 1825. the religious revivals of early 19th century America coincided with a spike in asylum construction. "how long, O Lord, our Saviour, wilt thou remain away? our hearts are growing weary, with thy so long delay."

this is the land where the Prophet Joseph Smith walked out of the
woods with the one true religion as revealed to him by a 1,000-year-
old angel with the name of Moroni. while the Millerites were taking
their charts and tents on the road and describing the Theories
of Last Things to enthusiastic audiences up and down the Erie
canal, a young diviner named Joseph Smith was brewing his own
genesis. in these days many took it as fact that the hills were packed
with buried Indian treasure. Smith came from a family of "money
diggers" and "glass-lookers," his father—a Millerite himself—and
uncle were diviners. young Smith's preferred tool was a seer stone,
an occult gewgaw popular at the time. not long after being arrested
and accused of disorderly conduct and con artistry for using his
"peep stone" to locate buried treasure, Moroni appeared to Smith,
directing him to rekindle a more primitive Christianity. Smith's
reveal is well known: he was directed to a hill in Palymyra where a
series of golden plates covered with hieroglyphs were made known
to him. after taking the plates back home Smith translated them
by stuffing his face into his hat into which he'd dropped his peep
stone—"the Urim and Thummim"—and channeled for days while
his wife took dictation. the Book of Mormon was born.

here is where Father John Humphrey Noyes, the "Modern Abraham"
and spiritual leader of a new tribe of "Bible Communists," designed
a thriving community (peaking at around 300 members and lasting
several decades) where marriage was "complex" and with multiple
partners, birth control was encouraged, eugenics promoted through
"scientific breeding," labor shared equally among the sexes, and
women got to wear pants beneath their dresses. as a young man
Noyes drank considerably, eating lots of tobacco and craving chili
peppers. afterwards he voiced the opinion that the second coming
had already occurred back in AD 70 and our obligation was now

to duplicate heavenly life on earth. since marriage did not exist in the afterlife, intimate engagements proliferated there, and so those who were blessed, already perfect in the eyes of god, should do likewise here on earth. by the late 1840s Noyes had established the Oneida community, where love for just one person was considered idolatrous, and so sexual relations with other members of the community were encouraged. so as to avoid unwanted pregnancies and spare the torment of women having their babies die during or after childbirth, men practiced coitus reservatus. adolescent boys were "trained" by being paired with postmenopausal women, and older men adept in self-control initiated virgins twelve and up. they called these "interviews." Noyes promoted a form of eugenics called stirpiculture, matching ideal parental specimens with one another to produce more perfect progeny. when children came along they belonged to the community, not the biological mother. the "sickly family" love women were wont to display towards their babies—"philoprogenitiveness"—was considered excessive and unholy, it getting in the way of loving one's god. in 1881 the Oneida community dissolved after nearly three successful decades, eventually reborn as a mousetrap factory.

it was in the burnt-over district where American spiritualism was born, starting in a Hydesville cottage where eleven- and fifteen-year-old sisters snapped their toe joints and bounced apples tied to strings, yo-yo like, across upstairs floorboards, fooling parents and neighbors downstairs that these were messages from the dead that only the girls could translate. the sisters even claimed to have heard buckets of coagulated blood poured across the floors of their home. channeling and mesmerism soon spread like a contagion in neighboring towns. in 1850 close to one hundred mediums had set up camp in Auburn, not far from Hydesville, and conveyed their messages in automatic writing, slate writing, and table raising. they

spoke in the voices of swearing drunken sailors, oversexed male
suitors, and Indian braves. (since those further up the hierarchy
of Spheres—Christ, for example—were too far out of reach, one
had to settle for those occupying baser positions in the afterlife). at
séances the attendees watched bells hover in the air, felt spirit hands
tickle their legs and nether regions, and suffered fruit baskets being
placed atop their foreheads. ectoplasm spilled from the noses, ears,
and mouths of mediums; ectoplasmic hands and feet sprouted from
navels.

John Spear, a spiritualist inspired by the Fox sisters and specializing
in "impressions," received thousands of pages of celestial
information sent to him from the Association of Beneficents, a club
of sorts in the spirit world. during the mid 1850s he founded the
Harmonia Community near Kiantone Creek where colonists were
to renounce property, live in octagonal houses, drink water only
from magic springs, and dig for buried treasure. instructed by a kind
of spirit community calling itself the Association of Electric-Izers,
Spears invented what he called a perpetual motion machine that had
to be jump-started by the "Mary of the New Dispensation," a woman
of spiritual intelligence who could nurse the machine into action
with her touch. no one, Spear included, could explain what the
machine actually did, but people called it Heaven's Last Gift to Man,
the Philosopher's Stone, the Art of All Arts, and the Physical Savior.
while on display in a building in Randolph, New York, an angry mob
smashed and scattered the machine throughout the town. a wealth
of journals, newspapers, pamphlets, and bulletins were in circulation
at this time, all devoted to mesmerism, electricity, spiritualism,
and news from the dead, with titles like The Spiritual Telegraph,
Christian Spiritualist, the Religio-Philosophical Journal, Messages
from the Superior State, The Clairvoyant Family Physician.

across New York state the less scandalous utopian fantasies of social architect Charles Fourier manifested in a number of brief Fourierian phalanxes. Fourier advocated polymorphous sexual engagements, looked forward to the day when domestic "anti-sharks" would swim in the sea, and predicted that humans would one day evolve into a race of tailed men with eyes sprouting at the tips of those tails. but it was his visionary philosophy of labor based upon an individual's private desires and harmonious collective living arrangements that many Americans found attractive. these "phalanxes" were short-lived but at least thirty of them popped up between Maine and Ohio, a number scattered throughout upstate New York.

> this is the region where Cyrus Teed (a distant cousin of Joseph Smith), engaged in his electro-alchemical experiments after receiving a vision from the Mother/Bride, she of the "matchless finger nails" who taught Teed that the earth was a hollow orb turned inside out, a seventeen-layered concave shell containing humanity and all of the cosmos. the universe was closed, sealed forever within this grand sphere, a cosmogony finite and knowable, at the center of which spun the sun, a little "heart-shaped disc." Teed became Koresh, the second coming of Christ, and preached Koreshanity, which promoted celibacy even though Koresh lived with a woman he called the "Pre-Eminent." although Teed's followers in New York state numbered only five, near the end of the 19th century a hundred Koreshans followed him to the navel of this "Cosmogonic Egg," establishing a village on the southwest coast of Florida.

*

these utopianist fancies are in stark contrast to the household my mother grew up in. like a lawn sprouting exotic mushrooms and toadstools, and in the center a patch of black soil where nothing will grow. I have wanted so much, especially since finding that generational link to the Public Universal Friend, to identify further strains running through the family echoing the spiritual enlightenments of the area's past, some connective tissue to those historical and at times hysterical passions focused on engineering pockets of paradise on earth. how disappointing to find that, here where a century before the land had been burnt-over with the most imaginative fires for spiritual deliverance, the operative imagination in my mother's house on East Elm Street in Penn Yan in the late 1930s and 40s was fixated on a different kind of burning altogether.

her worst memory is of the night her house caught fire and what her mother did afterwards. from her journal:

From my second story window I follow the red lights of the fire truck with my eyes. Everyone in the house is outside. I am on the inside. The fire, which is in the chimney behind my bedroom wall, I can hear it sighing. Mother, who had to pass my doorway in order to go downstairs, is outside. My door is locked.

They are all outside, looking up at the building. I am on the second floor looking out of my window. Amid the confusion a fireman spots my face. I am knocking on the windowpane. I might have turned on my light so that they could see me. He climbs the ladder, pulls me out of the window, carries me back down and sets me on the front lawn. I remember walking across the street to stand with a neighbor. [Where were your mother and grandparents?] I don't know. Not with me. While telling you this I can actually feel and hear the gravel under my bare feet as I cross that road.

the next night she awoke to find her mother leaning over her in the dark with a lit candle. she's whispering, sort of singing: *You don't have to be afraid of fire, there's nothing to be afraid of.* and she's waving the candle back and forth, over her face, like a hypnotist, as the hot wax drips into her hair, cheeks.

*

Jemima Wilkinson, during one of her sermons: "the day shall burn as an oven, and all the proud, yea and all that do wickedly, shall [be] stubble, and that day that cometh shall burn them up saith the Lord of Hosts."

the trajectories, the divergences. the Publick Universal Friend with her beneficent teachings, her attention to female children. an ancestor like my Eleazor Ingraham turning his life over to a proto-feminist cult. the currents of utopian spiritual design that blazed across this landscape, strange, at times comical, sometimes oppressive, measures of an indigenous people driven to rewrite the world in primordial hand, making it freer, holier, more visceral than what they had inherited. then, generations later, my mother's dark grandfather and her misbegotten parents, the family sickness. reversed yet again through my own parents.

surely I am making too much of these connections, imposing my fetish for links and connections too severely across this mosaic of history and memory. still, what becomes of these flows and reversals? which identities last, which philosophies wither? is there compensation? retribution of some kind? or is it just one life, one generation after the other, meandering wherever they may, toward enlightenment or misery?

was Wilkinson right? are people like my grandmother burning now below? is she paying for her mission to remove the child from her child? such punishments have no place in my own predilections of afterlife possibilities. but I'm no more an authority than any of the others who concocted their endemic cosmologies and metaphysics in this screwy, singular zone of New York state, with its blend of perfectionist and fatalistic communal alchemies.

perhaps the only authority we have is over the testimonies we spin and offer up for consideration, narratives of memory ineluctably tweaked in the course of their telling.

memory, a braid. one's interior recollections yoked to the local. these atavistic rites part of the continuum, the general weirdness of the region. the Finger Lakes a pleasant enough span of lakes and vineyards, but six generations ago a hotbed of concentrated spiritual experimentation by turns troubled, inspired, and just plain nutty. something in the water. like memory itself, genealogy, the historical record. in the blood.

STEREOGRAPH

Dusk cast the houses in shadow, flattening their projections. Blurred edges, like memory or soul, an event you turn away from. Yet I also believe that a sharp picture is not always preferable. Even when people come in pairs, their private odds should be made the most of.

Rosmarie Waldrop, *The Reproduction of Profiles*

on the kitchen table, old photos of that Penn Yan world before the war, my mother's childhood in black and white and sepia. next to each, Kodachrome slides taken by my father, from the 60s and early 70s, of my own upbringing, that world my parents fashioned. the pairings recall old stereograph cards.

the stereoscope was an amusement popular in the late 19th century. a hand-held device through which one looked at two photographs, each taken at slightly different angles so as to mimic what the left and right eyes would see. viewed together the pairings evoked three-dimensional depth. one finds them now in antique stores, vistas of Niagara Falls, patriotic displays, and erotica too, women in repose wearing pantaloons and gauzy lace, the viewer turned into a voyeur, the effect accentuated by having to peer closely into the viewing lens, like through a keyhole.

I have several of these stereographs. one shows a man with a young boy thrown across his lap. he is beating the child with a wooden plank, the caption: "The Board of Education."

the contrast between my mother's private child universe and my own could not be greater. unlike the stereographs, no synthesizing hybrids materialize. no picaresque landscapes or stoic families sitting frozen before American flags. instead it is the distance between her childhood photos and my own that stands out, the gulf between her macabre history and my own fairly enchanted one. the space my parents constructed for their kids was an ecosystem of construction paper, Classics comics, Legos, making puppets, fishing for pickerel. through some magick my mother managed to traverse the divide, left that underworld behind and in motherhood evoked new rituals. an alchemical exercise, to conjure childhood so without precedent. "as if spun whole from air."

from her journal:

the rain was making a loud noise against the window—I can smell the dampness in the room—she was screaming at me--making hissing sounds through her teeth—"yes—you are to blame—it's your fault--your fault--you witch—you witch—you make me so angry—they will say I did this—I hate you hate hate you...."

gothic as a Grimm's fairy tale. teaching her daughter piano lessons, Debussy, the girl getting it wrong. in a spasm of rage her mother slams down the long cover that protects the keys, the "fall," breaking her daughter's fingers. she would later tell the family that her daughter had crushed them while climbing racks of pipe in the garage. she refused to feed her daughter, so the task fell to her grandmother until the splints came off.

Simon and Garfunkel, Jay Jay Johnson, Kai Winding.
dad's obligatory Donna Summer phase of '75. Cosby,
Newhart, Jonathan Winters. headphones the size of
bagels. under blankets, under the dining room table. my
first record player, a hand-me-down from his ceramics
studio, coated in clay dust. I christen it with *Animals*,
Gilmour's trippy chords and pick squeals.

now that I've found somewhere safe
to bury my bone

the cat bites my mother's hand, it gets infected. that night a
show about bees—and suddenly she is off to the bathroom,
hand over mouth. transplanted to a day when she is
standing high on a ladder against the two-story garage.
summer, a hive inside the wall so fat and the day so hot
honey's oozing through the shingles. her grandfather has
drilled a hole, stuck in a hose in an attempt to flush out the
bees, but it's blocked by honeycomb. he can't dislodge it so
tells his daughter, my mother's mother, to give it a try. she
refuses, the task falls to the girl. *two stories up,* she recalls,
I remember clutching the rungs for dear life. reaches in up to
her elbow, it gets stuck. what returns is not the stinging
but her grandfather's voice, he who now has to *go and get
another goddamn ladder to bring down the kid.* that and her
mother's scowl below. *my hand was twice the size by the time
they finally got it out, swollen like a softball.*

at recess, I store the grasshoppers in my Peanuts lunchbox
with matching thermos. get home, hand it to my mother, she
opens it, bugs vaulting across the kitchen. repeating the joke
long after it got old. salamanders under leaves behind the
house, rust-colored things with ellipses on their backs. river
crawfish, river clams. fishing for carp with dobson and dough
balls. show and tell in kindergarten, I bring a caterpillar, a
fat thing with golden aureoles, crimson fringes. Mrs. Young
asking the class "shall we let Walter have him" and them
cheering "yes yes give him to Walter" and so feeds him to the
class frog. another show and tell, I bring in my plastic Ricoh,
my father had gotten it for me at a gas station for a quarter,
take a photo of my class. naps on braided rugs, hand-turkeys,
Kangaroo paste, mint scented, the kids used to eat it.

Peggy, her grandfather's dog, growled at all but
him. her only pet was Betsy, kept tied in the garage.
when she'd get loose the neighbors would phone,
my mother sent to retrieve the cow, would lead her
home by the tail.

parakeets, guinea pigs, guppies and angel fish, cats, and dogs,
always dogs, we could divide the phases of our childhood
according to the many dogs we owned. animal shelter rejects.
the abused retriever who could not stop shaking, the shepherd
mix that bit, collies with ingrown eyelashes and oozing ail-
ments. eventually a sheltie with no baggage, my father names
her after Walt Kelly's possum. satin-lined jewelry boxes, coffins for my mother's birds, she plants them on the riverbank.

taking out the garbage but the bag's too heavy, it
drops, splitting open, egg shells and coffee grounds.
this really made her screech, like fingernails on a
blackboard, she was so livid. tells the girl to climb into
the can then closes the lid over her head, *I heard her*
screaming as she walked away, I had to stay there the
afternoon. sprayed off with the hose later that day.

would bend to whisper in her ear

you don't exist
you don't exist
you're a nonperson
nonpersons don't have birthdays
people who don't exist don't get their pictures taken

ours though were major productions, she'd plan them for
months. took cake decorating classes so she could design
more elaborate confections. rocket ships, Baloo the Bear,
cowboys, dollhouses. would even design them after our
drawings. taught us how to grip the pastry bag, write one's
name in butter cream.

the symmetry of her punishments. when she was found with nail polish her mother would cut the girl's nails until they bled. when she was found with a razor her mother etched fine lines across her daughter's arms and legs. when she played dress up and broke her mother's shoe heel her mother burned the girl's shoes. food-related mishaps meant no dinner or being made to wear that dinner. "take those peas off the stove." but the pot's heavy and the handle's hot so she drops it, water scalding her, is made to wash the floor before seeing to the burns. carrying the buttermilk pail, some sloshes on the floor, her mother tries to make her daughter drink it but the girl holds her jaw shut tight. so she empties the bucket over her head, makes her wear buttermilk clothes all day. once she knocked an egg on the floor. *mother flipped*, she remembers, *began throwing all the other eggs at me, hard, then stirred raw eggs into a glass and made me drink it*. this last one materializing as my mother, forty-odd years later, was walking her dog, she had to stop to vomit in the grass.

her school lunches were elaborate affairs. pickle
and peanut butter sandwiches (not a punishment,
we liked it), celery with Velveeta striped down the
groove. pudding in Tupperware, hard boiled eggs
with a miniature salt shaker, Ring Dings, apple
slices with cinnamon and sugar. pears in yet more
Tupperware. chocolate milk. so much she had to use
large grocery bags sealed with masking tape, our
names Magic Markered on the outside. we were the
last kids left in the cafeteria, it took too long to eat
everything, made small talk with the lunch ladies as
they wiped down the tables. at home, kool-aid pop-
sickle concoctions poured into molds shaped like
bombs. you sucked out all the grape juice until the
ice turned clear. corn pancakes molded into rabbit
heads. gingerbread and Cool Whip, Dutch dill bread,
popcorn while playing Monopoly. dropping the spice
bag into the pickle pot.

the little lady ?

in the snow in her dress. her mother's shoveling the walk. calls the girl over, makes her sit on the stoop. shovels snow on her bare legs. makes her sit like that. recalls thinking *my legs will fall off.* when she lost her mittens her mother had her cup snow in her hands until the feeling was gone. another time took scissors to her snowsuit, cut it into ribbons.

forts in hollows beneath spruces. snow igloos.
would walk through the snow to bring us snacks
in lunchboxes, my sister and I miniature Thoreaus
luxuriating in the illusion of wilderness, behind the
garage, bologna sandwiches five minutes away.

she remembers echoes of sing-songy chants. from her journal:

> *"ssss" sounds. I'm waking from my nap thinking at first the radiator is*
> *hissing. then I realize I'd been remembering her chant in my sleep, I was*
> *hearing my mother, her ssss.*

one day she had a friend over, a rare thing. she's getting older, nearing junior high, and it makes my mother bolder. she and her friend are in her mother's bedroom trying on lipstick. her mother discovers them, there is screaming, the playmate runs home. she draws a lipstick map across her daughter's face. when she tries to rub it off some smears on the wallpaper. pulls the daughter into the bathroom, rubs her face raw with a cake of laundry soap.

a light year later my sister and I are in the Steele Memorial Library with our mother. we would bring Seuss and Sendak home by the armload. my parents encouraged us to write our own books, my first grade stories of evil magicians and talking dogs and lovesick men who went honeymooning with their lady friends. my father read Uncle Remus and Huck Finn to us in dialect, my sister and I disbelieving, how might a book make a man speak like that. the Remco Showboat they picked up at a garage sale, with its cardboard cutouts, my mother read the scripts and held the flashlight as my sister walked the characters across the stage. they built a puppet theater from a gutted television set. we would play "Dad Hides Upstairs," in which we would walk into a dark room and wait for him to jump out at us, we loved this. our ten pound box of crayons, the size of a small suitcase, and all of them broken, because it's okay to break crayons you're supposed to. drawings by the ream: psychedelic monsters, ghost-houses, robot-clowns. the word "WOW" because upside down it was her. when I was thirteen my parents remodeled my room, installed a four-foot black light and ultra-mod posters, glowing mobiles, groovy orange curtains. me, blown away by the splendor of it all.

from my mother's journals:

*then I saw it—lying open at the foot of the staircase—a small yellow
& green book—a lesson book for beginning piano—Introduction to
Classical Music—Book 2—I slowly picked it up & for reasons I know
not I walked downstairs through the dining room & kitchen into the den
& sat down at my piano—I put the book on the music holder—opened
it & very quietly placed my hands on the keys & within moments I
transported back in time Spiraling down thru the years to that day when
it began—*

*But this time it was different—It wasn't just a memory—I was there—
the rain was making a loud noise against the window & I could smell the
dampness in the room—It was a moment of unbelievable pain, fear—I
could not move I could not breathe—She was screaming at me—making
hissing sounds through her teeth, I could hear every word—yes—you
are to blame—it's her fault—her fault—you witch—you witch—you
make me so angry—they will say I did this—I hate you hate hate
you—It was as if she was standing beside me. My hands were filled
with pain—I closed my eyes & into my head came a strangely familiar
rhyme—O rainbow bright with all her light—shine down on me with all
her might—I said it over & over in my head—it enabled me to breathe
normally—It helped me not to cry or make a sound—it helped me
swallow the pain & fear—*

*The phone returned me to today—I got up—walked over to answer—
the receiver fell to the floor—I could not hold on to it. Moments passed
before I could grasp it & return it to the cradle—I was unable to speak.
The pain in my hands began to subside & I walked back to the piano &
sat down—this is something I have to do & I need help—Very quietly I
closed my eyes—breathe deeply—& asked for my guide to come & be*

with me—I don't know how long I sat there but very gradually I became
aware of a calming warmth surrounding me—I had been very cold &
had even put on a sweater tho the day was very warm—I opened my
eyes & realized I had been crying— tears fell upon the keys in front of
me—My hands were calm as I laid them upon the keys—the pain was
gone I pressed the keys & the melody that had been playing within my
head was now flowing down my arms & out thru my fingers & I was
playing quietly playing the entire melody from beginning to end— the
tears were still falling when I stopped playing—but they were not tears
of pain—they were cleansing tears

what my mom endured was twisted. yet perhaps no more than any of the illimitable accounts of abuse occurring daily to millions of people, hourly, each and any moment. every black eye, every pulled hair, every snapped finger, every cuffed ear, every burning, every lock-down. every fondling or groping, every rape, every day and night measured by neglect and humiliation and meanness and absence—every event utterly unique as they are common. no instance of abuse is ever repeated. every hurt its own discrete moment, scarring the universe as if for the first time. as sensational as my mother's account might be, the persistence of child abuse, the sheer historical momentum of it, more numbing still.

the term "child abuse" would not materialize until the 1970s. before that it bore the exotically clinical title of "battered child syndrome." not that historians, psychologists, and sociologists have failed to examine the miseries of childhood. Philippe Ariés argues that childhood did not exist until the demise of medieval society; before that children were simply miniature adults. he claims the concept of childhood irreversibly thrust children into a debilitating hierarchy, where they were destined to serve beneath the thumb of the grown-ups. the very concept of "childhood," for Ariés, commensurate with gross social injustice.

Lloyd deMause goes further. where Ariés romanticizes pre-childhood history as a time of greater equality between kids and adults, deMause presents historical and literary evidence revealing the sexual exploitation and physical suffering of children throughout all of history. "The history of childhood is a nightmare from which we have only recently begun to awaken. The further back in history one goes, the lower the level of child care, and the more likely children are to be killed, abandoned, beaten, terrorized, and sexually abused."

Philip Greven places not a little blame on the "Protestant temperament," our willingness to use the Book of Proverbs as a manual for child rearing, with its many references to whipping and applying the "rod of correction" to one's son. Greven points to Protestant fundamentalist manuals for raising Christian families, treatises that claim "spanking is God's idea," that "the scriptural method of discipline is simple and unequivocal: *the rod*." none of this was uncommon. Jonathan Edwards was preaching the following centuries before my mother was born:

> And let children obey their parents, and yield to their instructions, and submit to their orders, as they would inherit a blessing, and not a curse. For we have reason to think, from many things in the word of God, that nothing has a greater tendency to bring a curse on persons, in this world, and on all their temporal concerns, than an undutiful, unsubmissive, disorderly behavior in children towards their parents.

certainly children have had their advocates. even in my mother's childhood home in Penn Yan there were books promoting the virtues of beneficent child rearing. my great grandmother owned a copy of *The Mothers' Book: Suggestions Regarding the Mental and Moral Development of Children*. and my great grandfather had in his possession a copy of *What a Young Husband Ought to Know*, an 1897 volume published under the "Purity and Truth" series. both are filled with advice one would expect from this era: "an idle woman is always an unhappy woman.... her household duties are no misfortune, but a blessing." "there can be but little doubt that much marital indifference upon the part of wives is due to chronic constipation, which is so prevalent among women."

yet as absurd as these manuals are they also, in their own way, promote the raising of children in a relatively nonviolent atmosphere. even when *The Mothers' Book* insists that "punishments are absolutely essential in every home," it also claims that "it is undoubtedly true that there was far too much of the rod in homes until of late years. We would not, if we could, bring back that instrument of torture which, like the thumb screw, has had its day." punishment was not to be administered physically or when the parent was angry. instead mothers were instructed to whisper warnings into the child's ear instead of yelling, to discuss with children their actions, to dispense rewards promoting good behavior.

would that the adults in that Penn Yan house had taken such flawed guides seriously instead of letting them sit unheeded on their bookshelves. I would gladly have today's parents reflecting upon such imperfect passages than nothing at all. the need is acute: in 2009 "an estimated 3.3 million referrals, involving the alleged maltreatment of approximately 6.0 million children, were received by CPS [child protective services] agencies." The overwhelming majority of perpetrators of child abuse are parents, with women comprising "a larger percentage of all unique perpetrators than men." and the number of those not reported? and of children ruined on an international scale?

is ours simply a species still in its infancy when it comes to caring for its offspring? do we now find ourselves in an early state of evolutionary transition, and it'll take another thousand years, should we last, before empathy and sacrifice for the welfare of children are no longer bonuses but instead inherent components of the parental form?

I think there are two lenses required to put the animal we are into its contradictory perspective. on one side, people inclined to eat their young. on the other, those with an aptitude to convert past atrocities into adoration and patience.

winter, fresh snow on the ground, she has piled us into the wagon, pulling us down
Golden Glow Road into Stanley Woods, snow crunching under the wagon wheels.
spreads a tablecloth on a fallen log in a clearing, serves us cocoa from a thermos.
hiss of snow overhead, sifting like powder through the pines.

"I FALL INTO A WAITING TREE."

Easter bonnets on parade —
 Flowers blooming down the street —
And in my heart a wish for you
 For all that makes the day complete!

sing it loud & clear—
don't look left & don't look right
stand up tall hold up your head
remember now—or you are dead
you are dead—dead dead dead—

FROM MY MOTHER'S JOURNAL

after a year or so of these memories my mother spent a week at the Hoffman Clinic, a place where clients work with counselors to manage the effects of PTSD brought on by childhood trauma. mechanisms are taught for synthesizing the onslaught, converting panic feedback loops into harmless observations. psychological damage control. the days are packed with discussion, journal writing, visualization exercises. when she came home she was wiped out, her body moving as if underwater. the counselors reported that none had worked as hard as she.

it was here my mother became reacquainted with several of her childhood survival mechanisms. over the course of the week, what with all that poking in the minefield, an extremely early memory came back. she says it was from when she was two or three years old, but I'll say four or five, it seeming unlikely that one can recall much earlier than that. either way her father, this is before he left, is lifting her by the shoulders, his face red as a beet and spittle on his lips like tiny pearls. he's screaming, but this is a silent memory, she only sees his mouth move. then he's pushing her against the wall like a sack of flour. later they take her to the hospital, her ribs getting bandaged. she says her ribs got broken, but that seems too extreme to me. maybe they were just bruised. *it felt like a cage*, that's what she told me after having the memory.

when this one erupted she collapsed on the floor and it took three therapists, all huddled around, to coax her back. she reports that during this time she had no awareness of anyone in the room, no sense of anything save a single arch, a whitish, silvery enclosure suspended overhead. at the time it felt to her like no vision or manifestation but something real, a tactile architecture. she felt it difficult to breathe yet recalls a sense of being protected, stilled. she said *that arch wasn't imaginary but really real.*

later that same week she is sitting under a tree, a break between exercises, when into her mind the name "Jeremy" sprouts, accompanied with a resonant male voice that pronounces "we meet again." melodramatic like that. it's out of context, neither the voice nor the name holding any significance.

a year later my grandmother is dying in a nursing home, her house emptied for resale and my mother going through boxes of her possessions. doilies and dishware, stockings, egg timers. atomizers, hatboxes. and a print that had hung on her bedroom wall, all those years, a romanticized scene of rustic cottage at the base of a waterfall, banana peel birds riding a thermal in the valley.

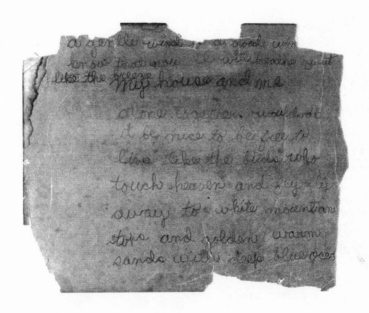

the picture is nothing special but the frame can be of use to my father, a photographer and high school art teacher, so she bends back the tiny finishing nails and pulls out the cardboard backing, only to find writing on the back, in a loopy, girlish hand:

> *a gentle wind is a good wind I*
> *know that now   I will breathe quiet*
> *like the breeze*
> *My house and me*
> *alone together. wouldn't*
> *it be nice to be free to*

live like the birds who
touch heaven and fly fly
away to white mountain
tops and golden warm
  sands with deep blue oceans

she fails at first to realize that this is her handwriting. or was in some prior life. she has no recollection of writing this, no memory of taking the picture down, removing the cardboard, inscribing her commentary. then putting it all back together again. secret note to future witness.

had she written it on one of the many occasions when locked in her room? did she have to move quickly? on birthdays her aunts presented her with small gifts, pencils and paper sometimes, but after they left my grandmother would make her daughter light those gifts in the burn barrel behind the garage. when the grownups were having their tea, did she use that window in which to write?

she searches other prints that had been taken from the house and finds other dispatches.

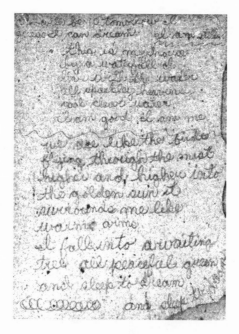

I will be 10 tomorrow I
guess I can dream   <u>I am still me</u>

  this is my house
  by a waterfall I
  live with the water
  all sparkling heavenly
  cool clear water
  I am good I am me

  we are like the birds
  flying through the mist
  higher and higher into
  the golden sun it
  surrounds me like
  warm arms
  I fall into a waiting
  tree all peaceful green
  and sleep to dream
      and sleep to dream

message in a bottle. lines of affirmation and defiant self-embrace, with a nod to Poe (my grandmother's favorite poet).

one note, from the looks of the handwriting, seems written in a younger hand, scrawled on the back of a maudlin portrait of a mother and babe

and on the opposite side:

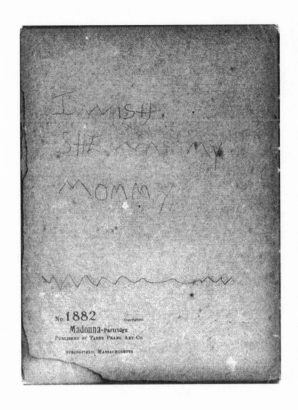

she finds an Easter card "from ma and Pa Barrow," her father's parents who still lived in the area. "Easter bonnets on parade / Flowers blooming down the street / And in my heart a wish for you / For all that makes the day complete!" like greeting cards made at that time it is a piece of paper folded twice in half. unfolded and flipped over, the reverse reveals a poem of sorts, each stanza contained within one of the folded squares:

it is raiNiNG iNsiDe
ME AGAiN BUt i
CLOSE My eYes AND
LOOk for MY
frieND. WHeN i
AM With
JerAMY i AM
WarM.

He SMiLeS At
Me AND tHS SUN
SHiNES iN MY
HEArt. JerAMY
tALKS tO Me iN
MY heAD. I AM
YeLLOW Like
thE SUN. it rUNS

iNSiDE Me
LiKe WArM
SAND. i HAVE
A rAiNBOW iN ME
i AM BLUE SKY
i AM GREEN GrAss
i AM RED FLOWEr
i AM PUrPLE SKY TO
AND YeLLOW ALL OVer.

GOODBY We
WiLL COME BACK
SOON.
    Judy — i CAN Write
MY NAME NOW
GrANDMA SHOWeD
Me HOW. i AM
       Judy
i AM 7 7 7 7 7 7 7
      7 7 7 7 7 7 7

Judy written in proud cursive. seven times the number seven, then repeated as if to make doubly sure she had indeed made it that far. as if driving the number home was an incantation, a survival spell. as if to say, you might burn the gifts my aunts gave to me today, you can force me to sit in the garbage can for the afternoon, you can push me down the stairs, can make me drink whiskey until I throw up, wrap dirty flypaper about my face, make me hold snow until my hands are numb, pour molasses in my hair, draw lipstick lines across my face, force my fingers through the rollers of the washer, cut my nails until they bleed, but you cannot prevent me from advancing. because here I am, I'm seven.

here too is one possible answer to the riddle of "Jeramy," the name and voice that whispered itself into my mother's ear at the clinic. some might choose to read this as some form of spiritual protector, guardian angel. such terms have little truck with me. I balk at the notion of "angels," entities that once upon a time might have been markers of a primitive magic but have since been drained of value, reduced to kitsch refrigerator magnet cherubim, lawn ornaments, bad television. this Jeramy, it must have been little more than just a chance name affixed to whatever power of sensory hibernation she called upon while being beaten or cut or burned or forced to drink some vile brew.

and yet, Henry Corbin uses the term "imaginal" to describe a threshold world between the physical and the imaginative. not an imaginary space but an actual world through which twelfth century visionaries traveled led by "angelic guides." Sándor Ferenczi, Freud's colleague, when working with an abused girl, was led to postulate the existence of the "orpha," an "omnipotent intelligence" that, in times of great pain, has an "anesthetic effect" on the victim. Ferenczi actually refers to the orpha playing "the role of the guardian angel; it produces wish-fulfilling hallucinations, consolation fantasies; it anesthetizes the consciousness and sensitivity against sensations as they become unbearable." perhaps this is as good as we can get: Jeramy, imaginal protector, transporting a girl inward to planets of warmth and color, muffling the actions outside. how many times did this confidante, this linked ego or overseer, carry my mother to some private refuge otherwise beyond her reach?

these scrawled notes dropped literally into her lap a half-century after conception, offering the first hints of corroborative evidence of the indignities suffered during those years in Penn Yan. shreds of a child's hidden autobiography. like straddling a fissure between parallel worlds, her older self stepping back into the 1940s to witness a child's shamings. woman and child regarding each other across the divide. it is the closest my mom has gotten to touching the girl she once was. I am sure she finds it a little creepy. these notes amplify the melancholy, augmenting the presence of this child who waited too long to walk back into her consciousness with her harrowing slide show splashed across the walls, her portrait of a mother who sought to efface her only child with an almost religious zeal.

what she did leave behind was the family kink, the poison that ran through my mother's mother, her father, my mother's cousin, her grandfather, and who knows who else within that line. the "family shame" my great grandmother made occasional reference to, gone now.

she became her mother's antithesis and fashioned a life arranged entirely around her children. maybe my grandmother anticipated this, sensed that her daughter would some day have kids and raise them as humans, not livestock. for as my mother entered high school, during the waning days of her control over her daughter, she took to calling my mother a slut, accused her of sleeping with boys, even went so far as to demand that her brother-in-law, Uncle Norm the doctor, "fix" my mother so she couldn't have children.

mom, whatever virus swam through your kin you absorbed it, let it wither. that part of the line ended with you. had you responded the way so many do in such situations you would have replicated what you witnessed and shaped me accordingly, and I in turn might have carried the torch and ruined my son in turn. as much as I try to turn over in my mind the phenomenon of this tragic girlhood I know I can never fully appreciate how close I, my sister, my son, and any who come after, came to having their lives written under the influence of your mother's, my grandmother's self-loathing, lonely fear.

a hidden poem dated December 26, 1946:

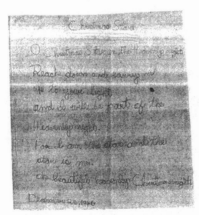

O Christmas Star in the heavenly light
Reach down and carry me
up to your light
and I will be part of the
Heavenly night
For I am the star and the
star is me.
oh beautiful heavenly Christmas night

the last of these documents reads:

> *Grandma got me*
> *my own tablet and*
> *2 red pencils. I hid*
>
> *them so I wont have them*
> *taken away. It's snowing*
> *out beautiful soft white*
> *flakes. If I were a snowflake I*
> *would be beautiful and soft not me*
> *not me not me*

and at the top:

> *I will write my poems*
> *who needs Christmas*
> *things. I will grow*
> *up...really really really*

I will write my poems

what needs Christmas

things. I will grow

up .... really really

Grandma got me

my own tablet and

a red pencils. I hid

them so I won't have them

taken away. Its snowing

out beautiful soft white

BORNING HOUSE

There is remembrance, and communion, altogether human and unhallowed. For families will not be broken. Curse and expel them, send their children wandering, drown them in floods and fires, and old women will make songs out of all these sorrows and sit in the porches and sing them on mild evenings. Every sorrow suggests a thousand songs, and every song recalls a thousand sorrows, and so they are infinite in number, and all the same.

MARILYN ROBINSON, *HOUSEKEEPING*

at Foster's Pond, on the north side of the Chemung River in West Elmira, not far from where I grew up, there is a black willow that has seen better days. the core has rotted away, the trunk charred by lightning, or maybe kids lighting fires. from maps I've looked at it stands more or less where the Dead House in the Helmira prison camp must have stood, the building where corpses of rebel soldiers were sealed into their coffins.

one account has a soldier escaping by bribing attendants in the Dead House who placed him in a coffin loosely nailed shut. as the wagon leaves camp and approaches the cemetery the soldier bursts forth from his box and disappears into the woods.

one camp survivor recalls: "I succeeded in getting out from the clutches of the meanest people that have ever lived. It matters not where you put them, they are the same damned people."

where my mother as a kid daydreamed about disappearing into the cottage that hung on her bedroom wall, I wanted nothing more than to stay put. among the hundreds of pictures I drew as a kid, of bug-eyed dinosaurs and dragons with flowers in their stomachs, of whiskered cactus people and robots with clocks for torsos, sobbing multi-headed clowns and futuristic cars shooting down planes with oogley radar waves, there is a drawing of my house on 228 Golden Glow Drive. nothing surreal about it. Just your average little home seen through a five-year-old's eyes. stones leading to the front door look like little blastula. in college I went through a phase where I gathered these rediscovered childhood drawings of mine and reworked them in oils.

rural American homes sometimes had "borning rooms," located off the kitchen usually, reserved for birthing and dying, those most primal acts, and their attendant rituals. they were portals, these rooms, threshold chambers preparing members for their entrance and final exit. 228 Golden Glow Drive, the safe house where I grew up with its minor daily surprises and comforts, music and food, its concoctions and language, was my borning house.

one of the imagined tales about Jemima Wilkinson has her jumping out of a coffin. instead of waking up from a fever and announcing her new identity as the Publick Universal Friend, this variation has Wilkinson's body about to be lowered into a grave when at the last minute her form rises, arms outstretched, announcing her new identity.

if only my mother's reawakening had transpired as painlessly as these romanticized accounts of prisoners and visionaries leaping from their coffins. but the truth is that for her this reordering of the autobiography, the toll, the cost, has been dear. it has now been more than twenty years since her first memories broke through and yet her depression continues, a steady surge and retreat, subsiding, resurfacing. I wish I could say that things are good with her today, but the effects of trauma are far-reaching and complex. early in this writing I was naïve enough to hope that in offering this account I might bring to her some element of closure or relief, a gesture toward resolution. that has not happened. and my gathering of her memories at times has not been without bloodletting. these memories were cuts across my mother's understanding of herself and in telling her story I have opened them anew, repeatedly, a sustained act of ritual scarification she never asked for.

I realize that my mother's need to tell her family these accounts, and in turn my passing along this narrative, might be seen as a necessary part of the healing process. "to recover from trauma...a survivor needs to construct a narrative and tell it to an empathic listener, in order to re-externalize the event." in his book *Healing Fiction,* neo-Jungian psychologist James Hillman equates the case study with a necessary form of myth making:

> my story is a grey complexity of nuts and bolts, all the metallic tediousness of what went wrong and who was right, and yet in that case history is my image, my dignity, my monument. And it is in its history itself: my mother had a mother and behind her an ethnic ancestral stream; the son with whom I battle is today, and tomorrow too. There is no part of my personal record that is not at the same time the record of a community, a society, a nation, an age.

144

maybe so, but the reenactment here of her (and my) case study closes on a less magnanimous air. while I agree on some fundamental level with this understanding of memory as myth and as such inevitably the stuff of history, there are moments when I look back at all this and wonder, would it have been better simply to have not known. to have kept it all buried. would that her ancient selves, and the memories they dragged in, had remained deep inside. for the triumph of her account seems coupled too closely with a mourning that in the end mocks the label triumph.

and yet

on other days the photos in that generational stereoscope, those portals into gone worlds, reanimations of her girlhood and my childhood the inverse, announce their mutual reflections as something more than just antithetical testimonies of loneliness and communion. on the left, glimpses of her lost then recovered childhood, melancholia mixed with the occasional momentary escape. on the right, my own childhood history, miniatures of hereness, presence-saturated, with their minor elations captured in my father's lens. but beyond this study in opposites, of how a child damaged in one realm might against the odds surface in the other as a parental architect of quiet invention, this dance of return and excavation reveals some larger ineluctable pull, that weird impulse to stretch the temporal like taffy, looking backwards with one eye while focusing ahead into a present with the other. like the eyes of a chameleon, each one rotating of its own accord, and magically, unnaturally, the two views re-assembled, conjoined within their hybrid narrative. that that can happen!

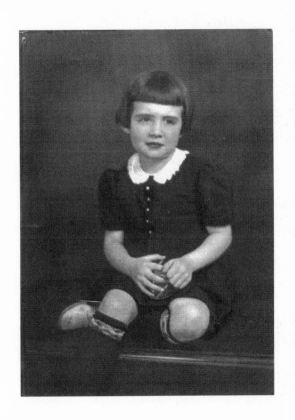

MATERIALS

return

"Somehow spread like smoke throughout the brain."

George Johnson. *In the Palaces of Memory: How We Build the Worlds Inside Our Heads.*

wax tablets, gramophones, switchboards…

Douwe Draaisma & Paul Vincent (trans). *Metaphors of Memory: A History of Ideas about the Mind.*

layers of octopi in shallow tidal pools…

David G. Payne & Jason M. Blackwell. "Truth in Memory: Caveat Emptor." In Steve Jay Lynn & Kevin M. McConkey, eds. *Truth in Memory.*

"stored in sensorimotor modalities, such as somatic sensations and visual images…"

In Jennifer J. Freyd. *Betrayal Trauma: The Logic of Forgetting Childhood Abuse.*

flight

"as unnatural as the paws of a seven-toed kitten."

Carl Carmer. *The Tavern Lamps are Burning: Literary Journeys Through Six Regions and Four Centuries of New York Sate.*

"war against the vegetables"

Allan W. Eckert. *The Wilderness War: A Narrative.*

"were bloody above the elbows…"

Max M. Mintz. *Seeds of Empire: The American Revolutionary Conquest of the Iroquois.*

"Large, dead-white circles had been painted around her eyes…"

Eckert.

"we destroyed men, women, and Children…"

Mintz.

where Indians were said to have heard booming drums…
Carl Carmer. *Listen for a Lonesome Drum: A York State Chronicle.*

"Extirpate them from the Country."
Mintz.

"part of their hair on—the other part taken off with the Scalps…"
Mintz.

a hundred "loose women" clinging to the army…, "There just ain't enough of 'em to go around…,"
"The size of the crops was incredible…," "Friday, Aug. 27. Marched at 8 A.M…"
Eckert.

around the time she ran away a ghost story is making the rounds…, "a white ghostlike shape…,"
etc.
Louis C. Jones. *Three Eyes on the Past: Exploring New York Folk Life.*

"Sacks of flour and baggage," "We never had so bad a day's march…"
Eckert.

in Catherine's Town an old squaw was found…
Mintz.

"Whether through avarice or curiosity…," "some extraordinary rude decorations…"
Eckert.

"I very heartily wish these rusticks may be reduced to reason…," Two were found and skinned…
Mintz.

the Indians had their own name for Washington: "Town Destroyer."
Eckert.

3,000 of these "Johnny Rebs" would die…, "I eat a dog," etc.
  Michael Horigan. *Elmira: Death Camp of the North.*

Elmira was built on the site of the small Cayuga Village…
  Eckert.

"All twenty houses containing featherbeds…"
  Mintz.

kin

Eleazor Ingraham, one of the original members…
  Yates County Historical Society archives.

"of very honorable and Christian character…," "She appeared beautifully erect…," Solomon's seal and skunk cabbage; etc.
  Herbert A. Wisbey, Jr. *Pioneer Prophetess: Jemima Wilkinson, the Publick Universal Friend.*

"love, charity, resignation, unlimited salvation, and good works"
  Whitney R. Cross. *The Burned-over District: The Social and Intellectual History of Enthusiastic Religion in Western New York, 1800-1850.*

"very grim and shrill for a woman," "peculiar dialect of the most illiterate of the country people," etc.
  Wisbey.

"made the Friend's shoes and 'done' that work for the family."
  Yates County Historical Society archives.

"Shinnewawna gis tau, ge," "second wonder of the western country," etc.
  Wisbey.

the memory stain

"Holy Mount Zions," "Here occurred very special spiritual feasts…"
   David L. Rowe. *Thunder and Trumpets: Millerites and Dissenting Religion in Upstate New York, 1800-1850.*

"no corroborated cases have ever been …"
   Daniel L Schacter, Kenneth A. Norman, and Wilma Koutstaal. "The Recovered Memories Debate: A Cognitive Neuroscience Perspective." In Martin A. Conway, ed., *Recovered Memories and False Memories.*

"the Achilles' heel of the recovered memory movement."
   Richard Ofshe and Ethan Watters. *Making Monsters: False Memories, Psychotherapy, and Sexual Hysteria.*

(a term which, like "recovered memory therapy,"…)
   Jennifer J. Freyd. Qtd. in Richard J. McNally *Remembering Trauma.*

"Unlike survivors of wars or earthquakes…"
   Susan J. Brison. *Aftermath: Violence and the Remaking of a Self.*

critics of "recovered memory therapy" are less concerned…
   D. Stephen Lindsay. "Contextualizing and Clarifying Criticisms of Memory Work in Psychotherapy." In Kathy Pezdek and William P. Banks, eds. *The Recovered Memory/ False Memory Debate.*

such reservations are warranted as studies document….
   Richard J. McNally. *Remembering Trauma.*

my mother's PTSD symptoms…
   DSM IV. 1994. Diagnostic and Statistical Manual of Mental Disorders. 4th ed. Washington, DC: 1994. For more on diagnosis and criteria information on Posttraumatic Stress Disorder see http://www.mental-health-today.com/ptsd/dsm.htm.

incredible testimonies, sensational media reports, aggressive prosecution...

See McNally for an overview.

"So far, no one we've talked to thought...," "If you don't remember your abuse...," "If you are unable to remember any specific instances..."

Elle Bass & Laura Davis. *The Courage to Heal: A Guide for Women Survivors of Child Sexual Abuse.*

for Bass and Davis, the symptoms of unrealized sexual abuse are so inclusive...

Summarized in Mark Pendergrast. *Victims of Memory: Incest Accusations and Shattered Lives.*

as one research would point out five years after...

McNally.

when Loftus respectfully but insistently challenges Ellen Bass...

Elizabeth Loftus & Katherine Ketcham. *The Myths of Repressed Memory: False Memories and Allegation of Sexual Abuse.*

"the options for those taking sides in this debate are quite unambiguous..."

Ofshe and Watters.

this divisive rhetoric has diminished in recent years...

See Robert A. Baker, ed., *Child Sexual Abuse and False Memory Syndrome*; Michael M. Grunebert & Douglas J. Herrmann, "Practical Truths in Memory," in Jay Lynn & Kevin M. McConkey, eds., *Truth in Memory*; D. Stephen Lindsay, "Depolarizing Views on Recovered Memory Experiences," also in Lynn & McConkey; Kathy Pezdek & William P. Banks, eds. *The Recovered Memory/False Memory Debate*; Daniel L. Schacter, "Memory Wars," *Scientific American*, April 1995; Daniel L. Schacter, Wilma Koutstaal, & Kenneth A. Norman, "Can Cognitive Neuroscience Illuminate the Nature of Traumatic Childhood Memories?" In Linda M. Williams & Victoria L. Banyard, eds., *Trauma and Memory.*

"a more balanced approach, we believe, is to acknowledge that society faces two serious problems..."

Mitchell L. Eisen, Gail S. Goodman, Jianjian Qin, & Suzanne L. Davis. "Memory and Suggestibility in Maltreated Children: New Research Relevant to Evaluating Allegations of Abuse." In Lynn & McConkey.

in particular, researchers have called for greater emphasis on an individual, case-by-case method...

Michael Yapko. "The Troublesome Unknowns about Trauma and Recovered Memories." In Conway.

claims that there are "over 1 million cases of 'recovered memories' each year"

Pendergrast.

...have been shown to be greatly exaggerated.

David Calof, "Facing the Truth About False Memory," in Robert A. Baker, ed., *Child Sexual Abuse and False Memory Syndrome*; Christine A. Courtois, "Delayed Memories of Child Sexual Abuse: Critique of the Controversy and Clinical Guidelines," in Conway.

separate communities that don't necessarily share the same training, goals, or discourse...

Christine A. Courtois, in Conway; Judith L. Alpert, "Professional Practice, Psychological Science, and the Recovered Memory Debate," in Pezdek and Banks.

"it is fair to say that the high levels of interest in memory failings..."

Chris R. Brewin & Bernice Andrews. "Reasoning About Repression: Inferences from Clinical and Experimental Date." In Conway.

most of all, skeptics of false memory have been reluctant....

Freyd, *Betrayal Trauma*; Schacter, "Memory Wars."

"there have also been documented cases of traumatic amnesia…"

Reinder Van Til. *Lost Daughters: Recovered Memory Therapy and the People It Hurts.*

patients with PTSD re-experience traumatic memories in a variety of forms...
McNally.

another study suggests that the more trauma a child experiences...
Lenore Terr, "Childhood Traumas: An Outline and Overview," *American Journal of Psychiatry,* cited in McNally & Kihlstrom, "Suffering from Reminiscences," in Conway.

"It is proposed here that there is a logic to amnesia for childhood abuse...."
Jennifer J. Freyd, "Betrayal Trauma: Traumatic Amnesia as an Adaptive Response to Childhood Abuse." *Ethics and Behavior,* 1994.

there are documented cases where people have corroborated their recovered memories of abuse.
Daniel L. Schacter, Wilma Koutstaal, & Kenneth A. Norman, "Can Cognitive Neuroscience Illuminate the Nature of Traumatic Childhood Memories?" In Linda M. Williams & Victoria L. Banyard, eds., *Trauma and Memory*; Jonathan W. Schooler, Miriam Bendiksen, & Zara Ambadar, "Taking the Middle Line: Can We Accommodate Both Fabricated and Recovered Memories of Sexual Abuse?" in Conway. Recovered Memory Project http://www.brown.edu/Departments/Taubman_Center/Recovmem/archive.html

rebirthing rituals and inverse baptisms...
Martin H. Katchen & David K. Sakheim. "Satanic Beliefs and Practices." In *Out of Darkness: Exploring Satanism and Ritual Abuse.* Eds. David K. Sakheim & Susan E. Devine.

burnt

"for whatever reason, the New York descendants of the Puritans...," "excitements"
Whitney R. Cross. *The Burned-over District: The Social and Intellectual History of Enthusiastic Religion in Western New York, 1800-1850.*

"There is an over-all, one-of-a-kind nonesuchness…"
> Carl Carmer. *The Tavern Lamps are Burning: Literary Journeys Through Six Regions and Four Centuries of New York Sate.*

"here is nothing to which the minds of good men…," "go-outers," "Genesee Fever," "nervous fever," "wake up these stupid sleeping ministers…," "emotionalized culture"
> Cross.

"inner space"
> Ronald L. Numbers & and Jonathan M. Butler, eds. *The Disappointed: Millerism and Millenarianism in the Nineteenth Century.*

"serpentine silvery colored belt," "meat and blood"
> David L. Rowe. *Thunder and Trumpets: Millerites and Dissenting Religion in Upstate New York, 1800-1850.*

"praeternatural happenings," "flying Goose-shot," "peels and beesoms"
> George Lincoln Burr, ed. *Narratives of the Witchcraft Cases 1648-1706.*

the early Penn Yan was called Pandemonium
> conversation with Idelle Dillon, Director, Yates County Genealogical and Historical Society, Sept. 18, 1997.

"alcohol in the stomach could be ignited," "hairs coming alive," hemorrhoid sufferers and horse chestnuts"
> Cross.

"seven-foot skeletons…"
> Mason Winfield. *Shadows of the Western Door: Haunted Sites and Ancient Mysteries of Upstate New York.*

"stubborn folk who recognized no authority this side of Heaven," "they may well have been as little driven by outward circumstance..."
    Cross.

"storm center," "psychic highway"
    Lawrence Foster. *Religion and Sexuality: Three American Communal Experiments of the Nineteenth Century.*

"Messiah is traveling in the storm...," "feminine spirit of a bisexual god"
    Cross.

"non-trances...," "heavenly parents...," "Spectacles of Discernment," etc.
    Foster.

"the coming of the bridegroom"
    Cross.

"I see children of God who are alive then..."
    Rowe.

"a very bad house...," "uncivil conduct," "gods Car is moving forward..."
Cross.

"The Disappointed"
    Numbers & Butler.

"as to almost sever his head from his body..."
    Rowe.

"religious melancholy," "religious insanity," asylum building
    Numbers & Butler.

"How long, O Lord, our Saviour..."

Rowe.

"eating lots of tobacco and craving chili peppers"

Michael Barkun. *Crucible of the Millennium: The Burned-Over District of New York in the 1840s.*

They called these encounters "interviews," "sickly family"

Wendy E. Chmielewski, Louis J. Kern, & Marlyn Klee-Hartzell, eds. *Women in Spiritual and Communitarian Societies in the United States.*

"close to one hundred mediums...," John spear, a spiritualist...

R. Laurence Moore. *In Search of White Crows: Spiritualism, Parapsychology, and American Culture.*

The Spiritual Telegraph, Christian spiritualist, the Religio-Philosophical Journal, etc.

Ruth Brandon. *The Spiritualists: The Passion for the Occult in the Nineteenth and Twentieth Centuries.*

sexual engagements, "anti-sharks," tailed men with eyes

Mark Poster, ed. *Harmonium Man: Selected Writings of Charles Fourier.* trans. by Susan Hanson.

"matchless finger nails..."

Walter Kafton-Minkel. *Subterranean Worlds: 100,000 Years of Dragons, Dwarfs, the Dead, Lost Races and UFOs from Inside the Earth.*

"The day shall burn as an oven..."

Rowe.

stereoscope

"an estimated 3.3 million referrals…," "a larger percentage of all unique perpetrators…"
Child Maltreatment 2009. U.S. Department of Health and Human Services,
Administration for Children and Families, Administration on Children, Youth and
Families, Children's Bureau. http://www.acf.hhs.gov/programs/cb/stats_research/index.
htm#can.

"I fall into a waiting tree."

"angelic guides"
Henry Corbin. *Spiritual Body and Celestial Earth: From Mazdean Iran to Shi'ite Iran.*

"orpha," "omnipotent intelligence," "anesthetic effect," " the role of guardian angel"
Judith Dupont, ed. *The Clinical Diary of Sándor Ferenczi.* Trans. Michael Balint and
Nicola Zarday Jackson.

borning house

"I succeeded in getting out…"
Horigan.

"to recover from trauma…," "my story is a grey complexity…"
James Hillman, *Healing Fiction.*

acknowledgements

The idea for this book had its conception during a lunch conversation with Gerrit Lansing in the early 1990s, back when my mother's memory haunts first appeared. Idelle Dillon, Director of the Yates County Genealogical and Historical Society, offered compelling anecdotes and access to Jemima Wilkinson materials. I owe much to long conversations with fellow burnt-over native and expert Thom Metzger. Claude Hurlbert's support kept me going at a low point in the writing. Tara Roeder directed me to Ferenczi. Paddy Welles, my mother's therapist, straightened out some of my misconceptions. Don Byrd, Granville Ganter, Susan Kublin, and John Shannon were kind enough to read and discuss parts of the manuscript. Cara Hoffman and David Matlin offered enormous support—thanks for the blurbs! Pam Ferro and Merav Harris gave the book a close reading in the final stages. My sister Renee Owens read an early version and challenged a few assumptions, and my father Ron Owens gave the project an exceptionally thorough review, filling in gaps. Above all, thanks go to my mother, Judy Owens, for granting me permission to write into her life like this.

Derek Owens is the author of *Resisting Writings (and the Boundaries of Composition)* (Southern Methodist University Press, 1994) and *Composition and Sustainability: Teaching for a Threatened Generation* (NCTE Press, 2001). His lyric essays, poetry, and fiction have appeared in such journals as *Seneca Review, Southampton Review,* and *Ecopoetics.* A Vice Provost and Professor of English at St. John's University in New York, Owens lives on Long Island with his wife and son.

S PUYTEN D UYVIL
Meeting Eyes Bindery
Triton